Growing Up Viking

Fond Memo

Ieda Jónasdóttir Herman

Cover Illustration © 2014 Guðmundur (Muggur) Björnsson. All rights reserved - used with permission.

Paperback ISBN: 978-0-9982816-5-0
Hardback ISBN: 978-0-9982816-6-7

THE LEGEND OF THE ICELANDIC COAT OF ARMS

"SKJALDAMERKI"
("COAT OF ARMS")

Denmark's King, Harald, planned to invade Iceland and sent a magician to check out a way to do that.

The magician turned himself into a whale, and swam to Iceland. He tried to enter the Eastern shore, but he met a Dragon protecting the island.

Then he tried the North coast, but there met with a Gigantic Bird with huge wings that scared him away.

In the West, he was frightened away by a Bull that waded into the water, snorting and bellowing.

Then the whale-magician swam to the Southern shore, where he was met with a mighty Giant with an iron rod in his hand.

No matter where he tried to come ashore, he was turned away in fear, and had to slink back to Denmark.

This is the way The Guardians protected Iceland.

ACKNOWLEDGEMENTS

Thanks to, Del, my husband, and all of our children; Lucille, Del, Marian, Peggy, Christine, Myra, Jonathan, Timothy, Della and Heidi, who have been so encouraging as I've been writing my memoir. Also, to all of our Grandchildren, a very special thanks. All of you, at one time or another have expressed interest in knowing more about my life growing up in Iceland, which started me down this memory lane.

To my two sisters Sisi and Lilla, thanks for your input, so enjoyable to re-live some of our fun moments.

Ísafjörður

Stykkishólmur

Reykjavík

Westman
Islands

Vík

Iceland

Eyjafjörður

Dalvík

Akureyri

Lake
Lagarfljót

Vopnafjörður

Höfn

Djúpivogur

Reyðafjörður

TABLE OF CONTENTS

EPILOGUE

ICELANDIC LANGUAGE

Explanation of selected word endings

At the end of word like ----fjöll

----fell	mountain (s)
----fjall	
----fjörður	fjord
----vogur	
----vík	bay,cove
----flói	
----ey	island
----eyja	
---- jökull	glacier

EXAMPLE Eyjafjallajökull: Eyja - fjalla - jökull --- Island mountain glacier.

Pronunciation

Áá,	say like in	ouch - how
Ðð	"	this - the
Éé	"	yet - yell
Íí	"	eek - eel
Óó	"	over - no
Úú	"	loot - moot
Þþ	"	thing - thorn
Ææ	"	I - Ice
Öö	"	hurry - hurt

The letter "C" is not used in any Icelandic words.

What memories do we bring with us out of our childhood? The significant ones? I think we do, even though they often seem unimportant, unrelated to one another. Sooner or later we all discover that the important moments in life are not the advertised ones, not the birthdays, the graduations, the weddings, not the great goals achieved. The real milestones are less prepossessing. They come to the door of memory unannounced, stray dogs that amble in, sniff around a bit, and simply never leave. Our lives are measured by these.

Susan B. Anthony.
(Grandniece of Susan B.)

Chapter 1

Traveling the Fjords
to Vopnafjörður

June 1935

They'd found me! *I could feel the ground tremble as they stomped their giant feet and coming closer, and closer. I shot out of the cave where I'd been hiding and started running in total panic, faster - faster - faster... but then my legs began to feel like lead, I could barely move. Clenching my fists, I grit my teeth and desperately tried to run, but I was going slower and slower. My heart felt like it was pounding clear out of my chest. Then the ground shook again and I sensed horrible, bony fingers reaching inside the cave, ready to grab me...*

Startled, I jumped upright in bed, what a nightmare! Just then a jolt shook the bed. I waited a moment, all was quiet, just a small aftershock from the earthquake couple of days ago, I thought, as I laid back down.

Suddenly I remembered; *today is the day!* For a moment, I lay still, feeling the anticipation tingling from my head to my curled-up toes. Then, carefully, I untangled my legs from my siblings'. Rubbing my eyes, I looked at the sleeping kids.

Búddi was tucked up into a tight ball, his nose scrunched up against the wall. Sísí was on her back, with her hands clasped under her head, dark hair spread out like raven wings. Lilla, sleeping next to me, had her knees pulled up to her chin. Her, curly, blonde hair was in damp ringlets at the back of her neck. I rubbed the spot where her heels had been digging into my back. The four of us older kids slept in the same bed, packed end to end like sardines in a tin can, while Frankel, my baby brother, slept in Mother's small bedroom.

A sliver of murky daylight showed through a small slit in the dark-brown curtain hanging at the window. I swung my skinny legs out and eased from between the, cozy and warm, top and bottom duvets. The floor was cold and I shivered as my bare toes hunted for my wooly socks, not bothering to see if I got my siblings' or mine.

Quietly, I tiptoed into the dusky, grey-lit living room. The quake had caused the large oil painting of Gullfoss to hang slightly crooked on the green-painted wall. The copper pendulum on our large Grandfather clock swung with soft, clicking precision, side to side, *tick-tock, tick-tock*. Nanny Gróa's loud snore came rumbling from the corner, where she slept on our divan. The white duvet rose and fell as she breathed slowly and deeply.

Stealthily, I slid my feet across the wood planks. A small *crack* from a loose board on the floor sounded like a shotgun blast had gone off in the quiet night! I froze. My heart did rapid flip-flops... the snoring stopped. I held my breath. Then the quivering, snoring rumble started up again, a notch louder.

Nanny Gróa was married to Sigurður [Siggi], a fisherman shipmate of Father's. When both he and Father were out at sea, Gróa helped Mother with housework and us kids. She was a big woman. Not fat, just big; big hands, big feet, big nose, and a very big voice. She kept us kids in line with just her voice. None of us were ever spanked, but oh THE LOOK, and THE VOICE.

I grabbed a black, knit, shawl thrown over the back of the rocker and wrapped it tightly around my bony shoulders as I crept up to the window. Lifting a corner of the ecru-colored, crocheted curtain, I peered out through the dusty pane. The ragged clouds in the pale-blue sky above Mount Esja were streaked and edged with golden-red sunrays above her snow-white top. Grey, eerie shadows floated in and out of her crags and crevasses and gave the rocks a haunted look.

The long, gloomy, dark days of winter were ending; the four-hour, grey, daylights were beginning to give way to nights that were getting lighter and lighter. Soon we'd have twenty-four hours of daylight that would last until mid-August, and then the cycle would start again.

I looked at the ticking clock: four-thirty. I had a long wait!

Glancing down, I spotted the small blob of quicksilver in the corner of the windowsill. We kids frustrated ourselves for hours with trying to pick up the elusive blob. Father had poured the silver onto the sill after Gróa had accidentally broken a thermometer.

Yawning, I pondered the slithery lump then tried to pinch it between my fingers. But, it broke into pieces and scattered across the sill in several tiny, silvery balls.

I gave up. Curling up on the floor I went back to sleep.

I was ten, and school was finally over. My two, travel-worn, scratched-up, brown suitcases, and a bag full of books, sat by the back door as Mother and Nanny Gróa bustled about with breakfast. After last minute checking of everything and everybody, Mother crammed our pockets with kleinurs (twist-shaped donuts).

"Time to leave." Mother said, as she picked up little Frankel.

Gróa grabbed the two suitcases while Sisi picked up my bag of books. Then we hurried out the door that was never locked. Sísí dragged Búddi by the hand as Lilla and I exuberantly ran ahead. We all thumped down the stairs and came out at the back of the house. Running through the dark passage that separated our house from the one next door we sped down the street to catch the rickety Strætó that would take us to Lækjartorg center in downtown Reykjavik.

Several people were on the bus and few seats were available, except the backseat; adults didn't care for the jostling and bouncing of the ancient, dilapidated vehicle and shunned the back of the bus, to the delight of us kids.

"Head for the back seat!" Búddi hollered. Sísí, with book-bag clunking against the seats, Lilla and I rambunctiously followed him while Gróa managed my suitcases. Mother carried Frankel.

After a bumpy, twenty-minute, stop-and-go ride down to the square, we got off and headed for the dock where the passenger ship, *Goðafoss II,* was anchored.

I was literally skipping down the pier to the gangplank of the ship. The harbor was crammed with a mixture of fishing vessels of all sizes, both foreign and domestic. Their masts reached to the sky like slender trees in a forest while a variety of national flags snapped crisply in the stiff breeze. Raucous noise and the steady roar of ships' crane-engines filled the air as bustling crews loaded cargo, shouting directions. Swarms of seabirds swooped and screeched overhead. Their abundant, gross, droppings, splattered and white-streaked the pier.

Breathing the salty, tangy air, and smelling gasoline and hot diesel oil, added to my expectation of adventure. I was on my way to Vopnafjörður, and I was going by myself. After much hugging, kissing and admonitions from Mother and Gróa I worked my way up the gangplank among the boarding passengers.

Shivering with excitement and a little chill, I tucked my lopi scarf tighter around my neck. Yanking up my creeping wool stockings and smoothing down my homemade, brown cotton skirt, I leaned over the ship's rail, and searched for my family among the crowd clustered on the dock.

My two sisters had traveled with me before; Lilla, now almost nine had gone with me just once, last year, when she was not quite eight. And Sisi, twelve, who had gone almost every summer was now old enough to help in the grocery store owned by our aunt Þrúður, and would be staying in Reykjavík.

As usual, I could hardly wait to see my father's family. Aunt Þórbjörg, my Grandpa Björn, and, of course, my favorite uncle, Uncle Bjössi, whose given name was Eldjárn, my father's half-brother.

The morning sun was hidden in a sky that was now overcast, pewter-grey, with occasional patches of ice-blue showing through streaky, low-hanging, clouds. Snow-capped Mount Esja was barely visible from across Reykjavík harbor. The island Víðey, sitting in the middle of the bay between Reykjavík and Mount Esja, had snow patches on the ground, and the black slate roof of the lone farm-house was streaked with white, powdery rime.

With good weather, it would take four nights and five days to get to Vopnafjörður. I was sharing a cabin with a young woman who was going to Akureyri, a town in north Iceland. My sisters and I had always traveled by ourselves. However, a passenger or crewmember was aware and available if we needed help.

A nippy, northern gale rippled the dark-blue water of the bay. The seawater sloshed up against the black barnacle-covered pilings, sending freezing-cold sprays over the folks waiting to see the *Goðafoss II* off. I spotted my family who were huddled together to wish me good journey.

I giggled as I saw my two sisters running for cover shrieking in surprise when they were showered with the water. Yanking their lopi sweaters over their head they tried to keep their hair covered and wave to me at the same time.

As the ship blasted the horn in preparation for departure, five-year old Frankel screamed and covered both of his ears with his hands. Mother picked him up as Búddi, my mischievous seven-year old brother, stomped both feet in the puddles. His shoes, socks, and pants were getting soaked as he wildly jumped, laughed and waved.

I covered my face when I saw him stumble. I was sure he'd go face-first into the bird-droppings grimy water. Then I saw Gróa grab him before disaster happened. It didn't faze my brother a bit as he squirmed and tried to wriggle out of her tight grip.

Another blast and the ship began slowly to move away from the pier. I was waving both hands and hopping up and down as my family waved back, Mother smiling. Her reddish, light-brown hair, wet from the unexpected shower, fell in long curls to the shoulder of her brown and white knit sweater.

The kids were jumping and shouting at a fever pitch as were other folks gathered to see their loved ones sail away. The yelling and the hollering noises were deafening;

"Bless, bless!"

"Have a good trip!"

"See you in a few months!"

It seemed like everyone was shouting at the same time, adding to the commotion.

Frankel had buried his head in mother's neck and I could just make out his chubby fingers doing a little wiggle, no doubt Mother coaching him. My half-brother, Kalli, who was 14, wasn't there with my siblings. He was being raised by my Mother's sister, Aunt Þrúður and her husband, Jón. I didn't see Kalli often.

Mother had been married to a fisherman, Karl Ágúst

Kristjánsson, who drowned at sea when Kalli [Karl Ottó Karlsson] was two years old.

Kalli was very much like Mother in looks and temperament. He had light brown hair, sky-blue twinkling eyes, easy nature as Frankel and Lilla [Herdís, named after Mother's mother]. But Búddi [Björn], Sísí [Sigríður, named after Father's Mother] and I took after our father, Jónas. We had dark-brown hair, brown or hazel, somber eyes, but each of us quite different. Sísí, was quiet, but at the same time could be quite fun loving. Búddi was outgoing and lively, and I was a sprinkling of each, but probably more daring or foolhardy than any of them.

As the *Goðafoss II* headed out of the sheltered harbor, past the two lighthouses, out of the calm bay and into the open rough Atlantic Ocean, I watched as Reykjavik got smaller and smaller in the distance. How the Capital of Iceland got its name is part of Nordic History; Norwegian, Ingólfur Árnasson, had heard about an island in the Atlantic Ocean. After a bloody fight in Norway he left and sailed for this land. When Ingólfur saw mountains on the horizon and got closer to the land, he threw carved, wooden, pillars overboard and vowed to settle where his gods washed them on shore. The pillars were found in a bay where steam from hot geysers billowed into the air. Ingólfur mistakenly thought the mist was smoke and named the place Smoke Bay [Reykja-smoke, Vik-bay] the town is now 80% heated by natural, geothermal, hot water piped into the city, and is virtually smog free.

Although others, like Garðar Svavarsson and Flóki Vilgerðarson had found Iceland before Ingólfur, he is recognized as the country's first settler, building his homestead in Reykjavik in 874.

As we sailed past Garðarskagi, the Garður lighthouse and headed toward Vestmannaeyjar, our first stop, the green-blue sea became choppy, and the ship began a roller-coaster move in the waves. The ocean fanned out wing-like on each side of the bow sending streams of foamy, salty water into the air. I loved to stand at the front rail and pretend I was a figurehead like on the ships of old, stretching my neck, pointing my nose into the air and let misty spray soak my face. I licked my lips, savoring the taste of brine. [Nine years later, on November 10, 1944, this same ship I was sailing on was torpedoed just west of Garðarskagi. A German U-300 submarine hit the British tanker, *Shirvan,* setting it on fire. When the *Goðafoss II* stopped, against the Nazi orders, to pick up survivors from the tanker, she also was torpedoed, and sank.]

Vestmannaeyjar is a cluster of blue-black lava isles rising out of the water about nine miles from the southern coast of Iceland. All but one isle were formed eons ago by volcanic eruptions from the bottom of the Atlantic Ocean. The latest addition to this group erupted out of the ocean in 1963 just west of Heimaey. The new isle, Surtsey, is named after the fire-giant of Norse mythology, Surtur, whose mission is to destroy the earth by fire at the end of time.

Heimaey is the only inhabited isle in this cluster. As we sailed closer, I could see white, frothy sprays shoot high up into the air as the ocean crashed fiercely against the sheer, massive, grey-black, cliffs. Then it swirled back into eddies of receding waves only to send another booming surge against the rocks.

Thousands of seagulls, krias, gannets, puffins, and other seabirds soared in the cloud-covered sky. Some of the birds seemingly hung in the air by an invisible string. Others would suddenly dive straight down like a falling star, totally disappear into the tumultuous waves, and then come flying up with a wriggling trophy in their beaks. *How can they do that?* I was quite intrigued and wondered why they didn't drown.

On this tiny island, only about three miles wide and four-and-half miles long, ancient volcano Helgafell rises 741 feet, among strangely distorted, eerie formations of lava boulders, scattered about from her own long-ago eruption. Another volcano erupted in January 1973. It was named Eldfell. It rose 721 feet.

At the foothills of these two volcanoes sits the village, and like the isle, is named Heimaey. Half of the village was buried in lava flow from the eruption of Eldfell, which also threatened to ruin the harbor. The villagers took the unusual step of spraying ocean water on the flow, stopping it and thereby saving some of the homes and the harbor. Two volcanoes live on this small remote rock of an island.

Chapter 2

Vestmannaeyjar and the Trölls at Vík

The mournful-sounding blast from the horn of *Goðafoss II* announced our entry into the fjord, echoing and bouncing off the towering cliffs that sheltered the harbor in a horseshoe shape, sending gazillions of birds into the air screeching manically in fluttering frenzies. Starchy puffins, with their huge red-and-yellow, gaudy-colored beaks sat on the edges of the cliffs, sitting on numerous ledges and on the steep rock walls. There were puffins fishing in the ocean and puffins flying over the ship, baby eels in their beak. There were puffins everywhere!

I gazed at the knot of people who were gathered on the pier, suitcases grasped in their hands and boxes at their feet. As the ship slowly navigated the harbor, a few stragglers, mostly kids, were running down the unpaved, lava-cinder covered street. Fine black dust flew up and swirled in the not-yet-bright sunlight. I watched as those kids carefully grabbed a few wayward pufflings on the wharf and dropped the baby birds back into the ocean to be reunited with their mammas, who were anxiously swimming in circles.

Excitement escalated and folks began to shout and wave as we eased up to the dock. Passengers gathered at the portside of the ship as the gangplank was being lowered for those that were leaving and others to come aboard. All the while, there was the grunting and the hustle of the crew as they loaded and unloaded freight. It was a lively, noisy scene; the droning of the engine of the ship's crane, directions shouted as cargo was moved, and the clamor as folks shouted to one another.

This dockside activity was repeated, with various intensity at every fjord we stopped; women, men, and children were greeting the arrivals, others kissing and hugging goodbye; curious kids pushing and shoving to get a closer look. The large ship was a once-a-month anticipation, when stores would replenish their goods.

With much waving and hollering of "Bless, bless" we again headed out to the open sea and toward the southeast tip of Iceland, the harbor of Höfn.

With a book in hand, I found my favorite place, the bow of the ship. The air was chilly, and most folks preferred the comfort of being inside drinking hot coffee and Brennivin [fire wine], also called Black Death because of its potency. The story goes that when an old, drink-hardened sailor from another country took a swig, he had to run six kilometers to get his breath back!

Drowsily, I dropped the book to my lap to gaze idly at the coast and dreamily ponder the mountains and the glaciers on the mainland as we sailed by. I watched with quickened interest as Eyjafjallajökull and Mýrdalsjökull came into view. Both glaciers had volcanoes hiding beneath their ice caps. It was just a matter of time until they would blow their tops. Hopefully not as wickedly as old Hekla, who lurked menacingly a few miles inland, her perpetual cloud obscuring her top. In the old Sagas, she was called the Gateway to Hell. I shuddered.

Suddenly, the hairs on the back of my neck stood straight up, I could feel my skin crawl... I bolted upright staring at the sea-stacks out in the ocean between the ship and land. *Two of those stacks were from Grýla´s family, the worst tröll of all the Icelandic trölls, which tried to snatch a three-mast ship that was sailing in these waters! I'd heard how they tried to drag the ship ashore to Vík. Then the sun came up and the two trolls turned into those stone-stacks!*

Puffing out a deep sigh I relaxed as the *Goðafoss II* steamed full speed ahead toward Höfn and the *'trölls'* were swallowed in a shroud of grey, foggy mist. I shivered in relief as they disappeared from my sight.

The coast of the mainland was hazy but I could still see the majestic, panoramic view of the largest glacier in Iceland [and Europe], *Vatnajökull*. The glacier rose dramatically into the air, top barely visible in wispy shreds of fog. An ice boulder the size of a house had broken from the glacier, and came tumbling down Jökulsár. Hurling into the Atlantic the boulder broke into smaller chunks.

Mesmerized, I watched the back and forth fight as ocean waves pushed the ice back into the mouth of the river, only to have the river push the ice back out. The river won; I saw the chunks of ice being tossed about in the sea, and then thrown up against the rocky headlands as the relentless waves showered the black lava rocks.

Drawing my knees to my chest and hugging myself, I stared in fascination as Humpback whales' powerful spouts exploded like miniature Geysers, white dotting the Atlantic. Seals lolled about on small volcanic skerries and dolphins shot up in graceful arch, wet backs glistening, as a flock of screeching gulls hovered over them. A gaggle of honking geese added to the melee. I found it very entertaining.

In traveling the fjords around Iceland, this was one of the longer stretches without a stop so I thought this diversion was perfect.

The village of Höfn was small. Numerous fish-racks were scattered at the edge of the pier with cod hung out to dry, the fishy smell saturated the air. Krias [arctic tern] and seagulls clustered and circled above the racks diving down and pecking at the fish.

Children were so heavily bundled up in bulky sweaters, I couldn't tell boys from girls. They scrambled on the brownish, algae-slippery rocks, yelling and chasing the screeching birds that would fly up in the air, and then come back down, fluttering their wings and hopping onto the racks.

Small rowboats and larger fishing boats were anchored in a seemingly hap-hazardous manner. The small boats smacked the sea as they bounced up and down in the incoming waves.

A small group of men from the village had gathered to watch the activity on the dock. Some were mending their nets that were draped among the numerous, strong smelling fish barrels. Puffing on their pipes, they occasionally glanced at the horizon and murmured among themselves. Their pipes, clamped between their teeth, bobbed up and down as they spoke. Tobacco smoke floated in the air, the whiff blended with the salty smell of the ocean and the rank odor of haddock, herring and other fish.

One woman passenger came aboard and none disembarked. It didn't take long for the energetic and experienced crew to unload cargo. We left Höfn and headed back out.

So far the sea had been moderately calm, most of the time. But as the *Goðafoss II* made its way past the peninsula and headed north, past the island of Papey and toward Djúpivogur, our next stop, the wind became northeasterly.

On the horizon appeared swiftly rolling, dark-gray, ominous looking clouds.

Chapter 3

The East Fjords
and Íngi's Boat

Suddenly the icy northeast wind came barreling across the ocean, and the *Goðafoss* began serious pitching and rolling as the heaving waves became more boisterous. Some of the passengers started to get seasick and threw up over the side of the ship, before dashing down to their rooms below deck. But once we entered the sheltered fjord of Djúpivogur the sea calmed, the plunging lessened and folks cheered up, even though the air was quite chilly for June.

Djúpivogur was typical of the eastern fjords; picturesque fishing villages surrounded by tall, ruggedly eerie lava mountains that plunged straight into the deep fjords. Numerous brightly painted fishing boats were anchored everywhere, by the dock, near the dock, away from the dock. Red and black painted boats, white and black, green and black, some were peeling, and badly in need of paint. Others were freshly painted.

The air was filled with hovering, screeching seagulls and the even more raucous, aggressive, seabird kria. As always, they were greedily fighting over any morsel that passengers tossed overboard.

The usual loading and unloading of the ship took place, and new passengers came aboard. I became interested in watching one of them; he looked about twenty years of age, with a cheerful round, ruddy face. A navy-blue knit stocking cap was pulled over long, reddish-blonde, hair that curled over the collar of his black jacket. His grey sack was tied up with black rope and slung over his left shoulder. In his right hand, he carried a brown, beat-up, square shaped case, secured with rope, badly frayed from being tied and re-tied. I was thinking it might contain an accordion. Bjössi's accordion case was very similar. *Maybe we'll have a rollicking polka dance. Wouldn't it be hilarious to watch people try to dance while the ship tossed them around like puppets on a string?* I laughed to myself as I imagined the riotous scene.

Easing away from the pier, the *Goðafoss* headed out of the fjord toward the open East Atlantic. Turning north and stopping at smaller villages along the way, we arrived at Reyðarfjörður. Men and boys were in couple of small fishing boats, and a rowboat, their fishing lines trailed along-side of the boats. The men and boys waved in cheerful greeting. Some of us waved back. After the *Goðafoss* had docked, a couple of passengers got off. One older man took his time ambling down; no one was there to greet him, and a woman who, firmly, walked down the gangplank. Her black hair was pulled into a tight bun at the back of her head, a off-white hat, (I thought it looked like a straw-hat) perched precariously on the top of her crown. Black ribbon on the hat flopped up and down as she walked with deliberate steps. She carried a brown leather valise in her left hand as she steadied herself at the handrail with her right hand, and stepped onto the pier. She was quickly surrounded by an enthusiastic, young-looking group.

"She looks so prim. I bet she's a school teacher." I thought, as I watched the group walk toward the village.

As we left Reyðarfjörður, we sailed out of the fjord and skirted the eastern-most point of land in Iceland, a huge out-crop named Gerpir. Great hulking masses of volcanic cliffs reared up. Heaving waves broke furiously on their sides.

Powerful waters swirled up crags then hurled back down into the sea. Wide-eyed I gaped at the fantastic lava formations of turrets and spirals, poking tröll-like fingers into low-lying clouds. In school, I'd been taught that Gerpir had some of the oldest rock formation in the country, believed to be around 12 million years old. A chilling flutter crawled up my spine as I gazed at the grim black rock and thought of the massive eruption that must have taken place. I hadn't realized what I'd missed on previous trips, as this part of the fjords had then been traveled during the night.

A strong gale, again, was whipping up as we headed towards Seyðisfjörður, after which we had two small fjords to stop at. I was getting anxious. We had been in and out of numerous fjords for four days and three nights and should be on time, if nothing slowed the ship.

The *Goðafoss* rolled and plunged entering the fjord that was sheltered by the enormous towering sea-cliffs. The sea calmed some, and the ship arrived at the pier. Soon the disembarking and embarking, the kissing, shouting and hugging began. The crew was working furiously to unload and load cargo. As I watched the haste, I wondered just how bad the weather report was. I felt anxiety creep into my stomach; I didn't want any delay. We were so close.

Sólveig, who was "looking after me" on this trip, suggested we take a stroll along the pier. I agreed, glad to exercise my land-legs for a while. Avoiding dogs, fighting with the ever-present greedy, noisy gulls, we walked on the ocean-washed planks and made our way to an old, orange-painted corrugated lean-to. A red-enamel, chipped coffeepot, with a hearty steam billowing from the spout, sat on a rough semblance of a counter, made from pieces of driftwood. Several tin mugs and a bowl of sugar cubes were at one end. A smiling couple greeted us and introduced themselves as Ketill and wife Sturla, owners of the small Kaffihús[Coffee-house]. They offered us harðfiskur [air-dried fish] to munch on, hot coffee for Sólveig and a mug of hot milk with sugar cubes for me.

Wrapping my fingers around the cup, I carefully sipped and blew on my hot milk, wishing it was coffee. I didn't ask for any, knowing that some folks thought I was too young. Looking out the grimy window, I watched as four men and a young boy were working on a small fishing boat. It looked to me like they were preparing to sail.

"Hey Íngi, I hear the weather report isn't so good." Our host had stepped out the door and bellowed, as he buttoned up his heavy yellow slicker. "Not planning to go fishing, are you?"

"Yah, but it won't be a winter-storm this time of the year, snuff and coffee on me when we get back, Ketill." Íngi grinned and touched his black cap smartly as he entered his pilothouse.

Ketill grimaced, scratched his scraggly beard, and squinted hard as he stared at the grey-black clouds, rolling even more aggressively across the horizon.

"I have a bad feeling," he muttered.

Sturla, standing behind her husband, pushed wind-blown strands of auburn hair from her face as her left hand nervously twisted a corner of her long, black apron.

"I can't believe my sister would let her youngest go on that boat today; Ragnar is only ten!" Her brown eyes were shiny with unshed tears - I felt sorry for her. But children started working at a very young age, and most were self-reliant and independent. We knew fishing had to be done to put food on the table and the ocean is good to Icelanders. We also knew that it could be their cold-hearted, merciless enemy. My family knew that as well, as several of our forefathers lie at the bottom of various fjords around the country.

We thanked the couple for the refreshment and followed other passengers who had started back to the ship. My eyes followed the little fishing-boat that seemed swallowed up at times in the roiling ocean.

The *Goðafoss* was at the mouth of the fjord when Sólveig pointed to Íngi's boat. We watched as the waves pitched the boat high on top of a crest, pausing for a moment then taking a slow, steep descent into a swell and disappearing, only to rise so high we could see the red-painted bottom of the boat and enormous hills of water streaming off the deck. Again, the boat disappeared. Sólveig tightened her grip on my shoulder. I don't think I have ever had such a sinking, horrible tension. I held my breath. Then slowly, like rising out of a watery grave, Íngi's boat appeared. I blew out a deep breath of relief, releasing the white-knuckled grip I had on the rail. The *Goðafoss* turned north and we didn't see the boat again.

Chapter 4

THE Lagarsfljótormurin [The Monster Worm]

The menacing, low clouds, scudding on the northeast horizon blended with the surface of the leaden, heaving ocean. The *Goðafoss* began to seriously pitch and roll, sending a heavy mist of spray over the deck. Sólveig and I ran for shelter by one of the lifeboats.

"Let's go inside" she said, tugging my arm. I just shook my head, my eyes riveted on the huge waves. "I'll go and get us something hot to drink." Sólveig looked into my face, smiled and left.

I was so glad that my mother had picked this woman to be my "look-out". She watched out for me but at the same time respected my independence. Her neat, wispy, mouse-brown hair, and slightly squinty, faded-blue, eyes made her look very plain, but when she smiled with that extra-wide mouth of hers she had the sunniest expression. I liked her and knew I'd miss her as she continued on to Akureyri where she had a governess job lined up.

I grabbed at a rope as a sudden pitch tilted the ship and I began toppling sideways. My heart flopped crazily. With a spine tingling sensation, my mind went to my father. Last winter he had been a crewmember on a fishing trawler that was on its way to Liverpool, England. They had just passed the Isle of Man when a winter storm caught them. The ship sank. Seven members of the crew perished.

That night my mother dreamed that father came to her bedside, dripping water and covered with slimy-brown seaweeds. "The ship is down, I tried to save Siggi... " Then she woke up. Later, I overheard as a spokesperson for the Icelandic Fisheries came and confirmed her dream. Father was safe. He had helped a crewmember into a lifeboat and tried to save Siggi, Gróa's husband, but Siggi wouldn't let go of the death-grip he had on the rail. He went down with the ship and drowned. I had nightmares of perils and shipwrecks for several nights but kept my feelings and fears to myself. I was a quiet, somber girl, very independent and, at times, quite impetuous.

Mother had quite a few dreams of this sort and was somewhat sought after to interpret dreams. Women would come to visit and drink coffee. Then they would turn their cups upside down and wave them three times over their head, and let the coffee form various designs on the inside of the cup as it dried. Then Mother would interpret the designs and swirls to "read" their future!

Six years later, when I was sixteen, she "read" my coffee cup and said she could see that I was going to travel far away, across a very wide ocean. I had dreamed of going on a safari in Africa. *"Doctor Livingstone, I presume"* was one of my favorite lines. I could just see it; deep in the jungle there I am fanning myself with a huge palm leaf and someone comes up to me and says" *Doctor Jónasdóttir I presume."*

"Hot milk" Sólveig's voice startled me out of my daydreaming. I let go of the rope that I had been holding onto and reached for the cup, just as a fierce Nor'easter struck. A raw, numbing drizzle, a mixture of sleet and rain right out of the arctic stung our cheeks and chins, forcing us passengers who had been watching the raw display of an angry ocean, to take one last look then, shivering, scuttle inside, shaking our drenched coats.

The captain and the crew were now battling the elements in earnest. We could barely hear the yelling of the crew over the screeching cables and howling gale that blew high and low.

I ran, spilling my milk when running, but when I got inside the steward filled my cup again, and gave me skyr [yogurt] and pönnukökur [pancakes filled with jam and whip cream]. Suddenly, the plunging and pitching of the ship threw a metal coffeepot clanking to the floor, sending splatters of coffee on the walls, ceiling and floor. Glasses slid across tables while people were frantically trying to grab them. Flying forks, knives and spoons were clattering every which way. My skyr slathered a stool, but I held onto my pönnukökur, squeezing them into a gooey mess between my fingers.

Sólveig grabbed me as we all were being thrown about like rag-dolls. Men were uttering swear words under their breath, others bellowing and grumbling "It's first week of June and we're in the middle of a winter snowstorm; only in Iceland do you go through four seasons in one day!"

The shrieking of the wild, north wind, and the shouting of the crew was getting un-nerving when, Svenni, the passenger from Seyðisfjörður, reached for his case, and opened it up ...*it was an accordion!* In no time, his fingers were flying over the keys and pounding out a rollicking polka. There wasn't enough room for us to get up and dance, we probably would have ended up flopping on the floor anyway! But we stomped our feet and thumped our hands in beat with the music as we crashed into one another with every roll of the ship. It was a real neck-snapping time! Then we started belting out our favorite folksongs, if not forgetting the ferocious weather, at least ignoring it for the time being. This bedlam went on for hours and we were getting hoarse from all the singing.

All of a sudden, in mid-song, Svenni stopped, cocked his head. "Listen..."

It was almost eerily quiet. I heard the creaking of the ship, still rolling and pitching, but not quite as violently. The booming of the foghorn blasted out! *FOGHORN!* That had to mean the wind had changed directions, warmer air brought fog!

The men scrambled out the door, we women clambered right behind, and holding onto whatever we could as the *Goðafoss* plunged thru another billowing wave. We had sailed past Húsey, Borgarfjörður and were slowly skirting Héraðsflói. Ice floes of various sizes tumbled and swayed in the churning ocean. The top of Mount Smörfjöll was hidden in fog, but I knew that on the other side was the fjord, and the village of Vopnafjörður.

I was getting very excited until I saw the ice ahead of us and heard one crew member say that fishing boats were stranded in ice in the fjord. *What if one of them is Grandpa's boat? No, I'm not going to think of that!*

I began to pester Sólveig "Do you think we'll get in there? Do you think there's too much ice?" I was very near tears. I moved away from the passengers that were milling around, some glaring at the sea in frustration. I found a spot where I could be by myself. Staring at the constantly heaving waves, I wondered if the monster-worm, Lagarfljótsormurinn, had lost his way, and was in the ocean wrathfully trying to find his way back to Lake Lagarfljót where he had lived for centuries. We were not very far from where the Lagarfljót River emptied into the bay. Fearful, I peered into the tumultuous waves, wanting to, and not wanting to spot this awful monster that was known to bode ill tidings if it reared its back out of the water!

"EEEK!" I screamed and must have jumped up a foot. My hands flew up in the air. "You scared the daylights out of me!" I was so absorbed in my imagination that I didn't know that Sólveig was by me until she grabbed my hand.

"You're gripping the rail so hard your knuckles are white," she said. "What's the matter? Your mother said you've traveled the fjords since you were six. You must be used to all kinds of weather and we're past the worse. What is it?" Sólveig asked softly.

I started to tell her about the worm, but then realized she had answers for everything, even the unexplainable. I knew she was not a believer in trölls, elves, and hidden people, but *I believed in them!*

"The weather has been so awful, I just wondered if the little fishing boat at Seyðisfjörður made it home safely." My lips trembled, I was also thinking of Grandpa and those boats stranded in the ice.

"Yes, dear, all we can do is hope and pray that they're alright." Sólveig patted my shoulder. "Goodness, look at that soupy fog roll in!" She exclaimed.

The *Goðafoss* had slowed to a stop. I could now see Mount Smjörfjöll's peaks covered with snow. Fingers of fog were swirling thickly, reaching into clefts and crevasses of the lunar-like landscape. I could barely make out a few white sheep grazing on the incredibly difficult, steep mountainside.

The thickening fog shrouded the ship. Crew and passengers looked like ghostly spooks as they moved about. The heavy mist gave me a feeling of being wrapped in wet, grey gauze. Staring into the thick fog, I could see eerie faces; hollow black holes for eyes, long curvy noses, and creepy bony fingers curled for the grab. My imagination was in high gear as I backed into Sólveig, who promptly claimed I was soaking wet and would get my death from cold. I looked at her, disgusted. She had absolutely no imagination!

Íeda Jónasdóttir Herman

Changing my lopi sweater and putting on a dry skirt and dry, black wooly-socks, I watched for a moment as the clothes swung and swayed with every roll of the sea, then went back out. Breezy gusts had lifted the fog quite a bit. It was still very cold. Ice floes the size of grown sheep were bumping up against the sides of the ship causing scary, creaking-grinding, scraping sounds.

Uneasy, I watched as the tide and movements of the ocean caused the ice to sway, bounce and head away from land. Hearing the engines start up again and feeling the vibration, I hugged myself in anticipation. Maybe only three more hours and I would see my family again.

Chapter 5

The Fjord is Alive with Seals and Ice

The *Goðafoss* snaked its way slowly along the coast to avoid icepacks. As we rounded Hellisheið cliff and entered the fjord of Vopnafjörður, exclamations of unbelief rumbled up and down at the rails of the ship as passengers gathered in awe. *The fjord was alive with tumbling, rolling, bobbing ice-chunks and floes.*

"Oh look, the seals are going for a ride on the ice, isn't that cute!" Some of the women cooed.

"Wonder if there are any polar bears; wouldn't that be something!" One man muttered. The ship, or perhaps the noise of the folks, must have bothered the seals; they began to scoot off the ice and flop into the sea, their large, shiny eyes looked at us curiously, as they swam away.

The combination of ebb tide and flowing of the ocean was moving the ice pack to the mouth of the fjord. I followed one large mass with my eyes... would that one reach Færeyjar Islands? Maybe it'll get to Norway, and by then be melted into an itsy-bitsy piece? How long would it take a chunk like that to melt? Would the seals get back onto the ice and take a long ride? Would the ice just disappear from under them?

I was mulling this over when I spotted a wrecked fishing vessel lying on its side and half-submerged in the ocean. My stomach lurched, and I felt icy cold as I saw the exposed, black painted stern, waves washing over it in great sloshing gushes.

Then I noticed the Norwegian flag painted on the side. I felt guilt at the feeling of relief that warmed my body. This wasn't Grandpa's boat.

I was ecstatic when we arrived at the dock. Aunt Þórbjörg gave me a tight bear hug as I got off the ship, pushed me back, took another look, then grabbed me again, rocking side to side. I always felt special when I was with them. She and Ólafur didn't have children, they treated me more as a daughter.

Þórbjörg was wearing her blue and white striped nurses' dress. She had taken off her white apron and stiff cap. Her short, black hair had a two-inch wide patch of white hair above her left eyebrow and went back to just above her left ear. Like Grandma Sigríður's mother [grand-Amma], Þórbjörg's right eye was brown and the left one blue. She had easy laughter and great patience. She also was a very good nurse, and the only one in the village.

Ólafur was the caretaker of the sjúkrahús [hospital]. He was a quiet, rather powerfully built man that could, and did, handle any difficult patient at the infirmary. His grayish-blond hair was thin and receding although he wasn't old. They both were in their mid-thirties. His large, brown lopi sweater drooped unevenly below his waist, giving him a bedraggled but comfortable look.

Sólveig had been standing by, and now the introductions took place as we ambled to a small building where coffee was being served. When Ólafur heard that she was on her way to Akureyri to be a governess, he wanted to know the name of the family where she was going. It turned out he knew the family quite well. Akureyri had been his hometown when he was growing up.

Sólveig's face was flushed with delight. Until then I hadn't had an inkling of her unsure feelings about this post. After visiting awhile we walked back to the ship to see Sólveig off, she glanced over to the wreck of the Norwegian boat, then looked at Þórbjörg with a questioning look. My aunt nodded. "I have three of them at the infirmary. The rest we weren't able to save." She looked away, but I saw the single tear that trickled down her left cheek. Sólveig reached out and gave her a sympathetic hug as the whistle for departure rang through the air.

Grabbing me tightly she laughed "Bless, bless, elska mín [my love]." Then giving me a droll wink she chuckled again. "And don't daydream too much!"

After embracing Þórbjörg then Ólafur she swiftly walked up the gangplank. As she stepped on deck she turned, waved, and blew us a kiss. I was going to miss her.

Ólafur reached down and picked up my two suitcases as Þórbjörg was inquiring about medical supplies she was expecting. She was told that her box was already unloaded and at the warehouse. We walked past a couple of empty corrugated sheds so weather-beaten that it was impossible to tell the original paint. The warehouse was in better shape. The wood front was freshly painted white. A window and the extra-wide door were red-trimmed matching the red corrugated roof. Several people were milling around inside as we entered the door. Many started to ask about the survivors.

"Þórbjörg, over here I have your supplies." The roar came from a bear of a man who towered over everyone. His huge, red beard drooped down his chin and his fiery red hair stuck out from his head as if he'd stuck a finger into a electric socket. "How are the Norwegians doing? It's too bad, we couldn't get to all of them, but... " His voice was rough as it boomed from his massive chest. I cringed and snuck behind Ólafur.

"Scared the little one," he said. "Sorry. Anyway, here's your box, Þórbjörg. Not very heavy."

"Thank you, Halldór." Then she turned and looked at the folks that had been asking about her patients. "All but one is doing well, but I'm sure they'll all recover soon and be able to rejoin their families." My aunt smiled as she and Ólafur walked out the door. Little one, hmmp! I was big enough to travel by myself for five days and four nights. Well, almost by myself. I was no little one! Þórbjörg glanced at my kicking feet raising the dust.

"I need to have coffee roasted and ground when we get home. I'm almost out." She said that to Ólafur. I cooled off. I knew she meant that for me, knowing that my absolute favorite job was to grind coffee beans!

We walked past the white church where old Snorri, the bell ringer, rang the bell every Sunday morning; winter, snow, sleet or summer, he was there without fail. Every Sunday that I was with Aunt Þórbjörg and Ólafur we attended that little Lutheran church. Christianity was first started in the year 1000 in Iceland, introduced by the Viking, Leif "The Lucky" Eriksson.

As we walked towards the infirmary, I glanced to my left. The wide inlet of the fjord was still heaving and splashing against the rugged coast. Huge columns of powerful sprays shot up into the air, making the seabirds - especially the gulls - screech like crazy. Through the mist, I could see Smjörfjöll reach grandly up to the sky. There was less snow on her peaks than the other side where we had sailed past few hours before.

The steep, rugged, basalt-black rock wall rose high on our right side as we walked toward the house. Several rjúpa [Ptarmigans] sat on ledges in the crevasses, their white winter feathers beginning to turn a summer speckled-brown. Walking by didn't disturb them at all.

Kristján, the shoemaker, had a small house and shoe-making shack on top of that cliff. Finna, his eleven-year old daughter, ran out to holler and wave at me, her high-pitched voice echoing in the crags. I waved back and had to grab my aunt's skirt to keep from falling as I stumbled. My eyes were everywhere except on the road!

When Finna and I would go to see one another, we didn't bother to use the road, but climbed up and down the sheer lava cliff by finding a gritty ledge in which to stick our toes, or grip with our fingers. At times the brittle shale would break off with heart-stopping suddenness that sent our adrenalin racing, and momentarily scaring us half to death, but it was never enough to stop us from using the precarious mode of visiting one another, and perchance picking a few bird eggs.

I was getting more anxious as we got closer to the house-hospital, I couldn't wait to look around. I wanted to be sure nothing had changed.

The two corrugated sheds were askew from the earthquake last year, but still standing. I could still jump from one shed to the other! My mind went back to the earthquake...

Chapter 6

The Year Before, With My Two Sisters

"Hey look, Lilla, if we put flour sacks over our arms we could fly just like the gulls up there." I squinted my eyes to watch one bird standing on a large lava rock. I stomped my foot to see how he'd take off; spreading his wings wide, he glided up into the air, feet tucked under his body. Gracefully swooping in a curve, he came for a landing on another rock a stone-throw away. I could see his webbed, yellow feet come down straight and watched as he hopped a bit before settling down.

"Did you see that? We can do that!" I hollered. "See? When we get up on top of the shed, we'll put the sacks on our arms, spread them out like wings and when we jump, pull up our knees and fly from one roof to the other. Come on, Lilla. Grandpa and Sisí will be here later. Let's show them how we do this!"

I was already climbing on top of one of the sheds.

"No, no, come on down. The roof is shaking!" Lilla shrieked as small rocks began to rain down the cliff at the back of the sheds. I could feel the shed swaying and hear the clattering noise as the rocks pelted the corrugated sides. Frantically, I scrambled back down yelling, "Run Lilla, run, it's an earthquake, the trölls will be coming!" Then both of us were running oddly, as if we were on the deck of a ship in a stormy gale. Reeling and weaving, we screamed hysterically *The trölls are coming, the trölls are coming!*

Both Ólafur and Aunty came running out of the house, each one grabbed one of us and tried to calm us down, even as it felt like a giant worm was crawling under our feet.

"This is just a little tremor, and the center of the quake is miles away!" Ólafur said as he tried to calm us down.

"What on earth do you mean 'the trölls are coming'?" Aunt Þórbjörg asked as we hurried into the house. A few pictures were hanging crookedly on the walls. A spoon, two forks and a cup had bounced off the table and were quivering on the floor. A small rivulet of coffee meandered across the wood planks, from the upside-down, black-enamel coffeepot.

"What was that? What's happening?" The gravelly, querulous voice was that of old, blind, Olga, who had been in the infirmary as long as I could remember. Þórbjörg went into the sickroom and we could hear the soothing voice of our aunt as she told the old woman about the earth tremor. When she came back out, she straightened a couple of the pictures. Ólafur had given us some bread and milk and we were settling down. After a while, she stopped fiddling with stuff, turning, as she fixed a sharp stare on me, black eyebrows in a tight frown, not on Lilla, mind you; but *me* and said,

"I want to know about this nonsense of the trölls." Her voice sounded grim.

"Íeda has told me about the trölls and I'm scared they'll get me," Lilla said, whimpering.

Crossing her arms across her chest, she frowned at me. "Alright, out with it. Why have you been scaring your sister?"

She didn't even call me "Diddamín." I'd thought I was the favored child! I opened my mouth and then yelped and jumped toward my aunt who opened her arms to catch me.

"It's just a little after-shock Diddamín. Let's sit down."

The house gave a little shudder and a couple of cooking-pots clattered on the stove. A few glasses clinked shrilly in the cabinet. Then, everything quieted down. Aunt Þórbjörg evidently forgot to be angry; she hugged me and rocked from side to side as Ólafur comforted Lilla.

"Tell me what you've heard about this silly superstition" Aunty squeezed my shoulders.

"Uncle Bjössi said trölls live in those big, black rocks in Vopnafjörður." I shivered. "He said it was a recorded history in the *Heimskringlan* that the trölls first started here; the volcanoes opened fire and spewed them out. The trölls come out when earthquakes split openings in the cliffs. The trölls snatch children, especially the naughty ones" I shuddered as I buried my face in Aunties white sweater. I knew I was naughty at times, a little stubborn and did things I shouldn't. I was sure I'd be the first one to be snatched! I felt a little shake go through her body. Was she laughing? Anxiously, I peeked at her face. Sure enough, her face was all puckered up in a silent chuckle.

"My brother, Bjössi. I should have known!" She said. "This is quite a story! Honey, don't you know any better than to believe his tall tales? But you really shouldn't scare your little sister with these stories, and I know all about your outrageous imagination!" Aunty chuckled again.

"You don't believe the trölls are real?" I asked, shocked.

"No trölls? The trölls aren't real?" Lilla asked in a squeaky, trembling voice.

"Definitely not real." Ólafur's voice was firm.

I got off Auntie's lap. With my hands on my hips, I planted my feet apart, and with a pugnacious stare at her, then at my uncle, I demanded, "You don't think trölls are real?"

I was sure such heresy would bring the wrath of the trölls upon us! "What about the *Monster-worm*? Everybody knows he's real and lives in the lake not far from Smjörfjöll over there."

I pointed to the mountain range across the fjord. "He is just as bad as the trölls in causing bad things to happen. I've heard people whisper about that one, Aunt Þórbjörg!" My voice rose with indignation.

Uncle Ólafur tried to hide a smile in Lilla's hair, as my Aunt snorted.

"You silly goose, of course he's not real either." My aunt was unable to control her laughter. I didn't like this one bit. I bent forward and looked her straight in the eyes, wrinkling my nose, scrunching my face...

"Well, what about the ´Hidden People'?" I didn't stamp my foot, but I sure felt like it. I'd rather enjoyed the delicious thrill of fear that crawled up my spine as Bjössi would drop his voice to a whisper;

"Hush, listen, don't you hear moaning and wailing?" Then, curling his fingers into claws, he'd suddenly grab me and make me screech with fright.

Then he'd get serious. "Don't wander too far away from the ruts the horses and cows have made, Diddamín. They know their way, but it's easy for folks to get lost out there. When a thick fog comes up suddenly, I let Thunder take over and guide me home. Always remember, if ever you find yourself lost, let your horse, the dog, or even the old cow Rauða guide you. Take a hold of a tail and don't let go!" Bjössi was eighteen and, in between unmerciful teasing, he did teach me quite a bit about being careful in our remote, and strangely eerie, country.

Þórbjörg quit laughing. Looking sideways at Ólafur, she gnawed at her lower lip as she reached for me.

"I'm sorry Diddamín. I shouldn't laugh. You're right. There are some things one can't explain, but you can be sure that trölls and monsters aren't real. And you don't have to be afraid of them. People that believe in 'Hidden Folks' say that they are the kind, and helpful. There are many tales about these beings, how they have guided folks to safety after they had lost their way on fog-shrouded tundra." Aunty paused a moment, then with a serious look on her face she continued.

"I have no personal experience, but I do believe in being kind to strangers. What story did you tell Lilla that scared her so?"

"If I tell the story won't Lilla start screaming? She *always* screams!" I bumped into the stove as I backed away from Aunty.

Lilla let out a blood-curdling howl as a big kettle careened off the stove and noisily crashed to the floor, the lid banging away as it rolled into a corner of the kitchen and came to a quivering stop. We hadn't noticed how precariously close the pot was to the edge. Fortunately, it was empty. Aunt Þórbjörg picked up the pot and lid and placed them back on top of the stove. There were no more tremors and no aftershocks.

"Let's sit outside for a while and you can tell me the stories your uncle has been telling you while Ólafur and Lilla take some coffee to Olga."

We walked down a short lane and seated ourselves on a flat lava rock. The northern breeze blowing across the ocean was chilly, even though it was June. We both had on our warm lopi sweaters.

Taking my right hand, she rubbed it with both of hers. "I'm not mad at you, Diddamín. Well, maybe a little bit at first. It's just that I don't want you and Lilla to be scared of these folktales, and that's all they are!"

"But I've read many stories up in Grandpa's attic, and I asked Björssi about them." I argued. "He said they were all true!" I wasn't willing to give up my favorite daydreams!

"So what makes Lilla so very scared?" Aunty narrowed her left, blue, eye almost shut.

Rubbing the toe of my right sheepskin shoe into the dirt, I

drew little circles, giving Aunty a sideways, sheepish look.

"The trölls are full of tricks, and always cause trouble." I explained. "The 'Hidden Folks' are kind and try to help when the trölls have been mean. The scary thing is that the trölls snatch naughty little kids, so I told Lilla since she was the littlest of us girls; she'd be the easiest one to catch. And better be good or she'd be snatched for sure!"

Aunt Þórbjörg got up, brushing her skirt. "Well it's not nice of you to scare her like that. You should be taking care of your pretty little sister."

Ah, there it was. Lilla was the 'pretty' little girl. Which meant; she's 'lady-like'. Sísí had a 'head on her shoulders.' Which meant; she's 'the smart' one. And I was the tomboy, which meant; 'one of these days she's going to break her foolhardy neck'! I loved my two sisters, but I didn't like to be in the middle; not the younger one, not the older one, just there.

"I only told her that if we stare hard into the fog, or clouds, or the cliffs, we could see the faces of trölls and ghosts!" The loose scoria from the tremor rolled, and crunched, under my feet as I walked over to the cliff that sheltered the house.

"Can't you see this face over here?" Timidly I pointed to two black holes in a crag of the lava-rock wall. "See? Two eyes, a long, curvy nose and an open mouth with long whiskers on a huge chin. And why is it that so often we hear awful wailing and moaning all around us if it's not the naughty children the trölls have taken?"

"Now you've added ghosts? You are hopeless!" Aunty plunked back down shaking her head.

"First of all, that's not a face, just a formation from an old lava flow. Fog and clouds will do similar formations. Some people say they see a man's face on a full moon. It's all in the imagination, and you've got more than your share of that!" She

35

chuckled. "As far as the moaning noise, that's the wind. We have the wind constantly blowing through all the crooks and crannies of the volcanic cliffs. They do make odd sounds, especially when it's the Northern wind."

I wasn't finished. "Why do all the places have names? The farms, the waterfalls, the mountains?"

Þórbjörg turned abruptly and stared at me for a second, shaking her head again in an 'I give up' gesture.

After a moment, she said, "Folks have been giving names to places forever, something that has meaning for them or a description."

"Well then." I argued. "If there are no trölls, why name a waterfall Tröllafoss, or a lake Tröll Lake, or the Tröll Peninsula, or... "My aunt gave me a scorching look that told me I had gone a bit too far. I clamped my mouth, but inside I felt giddy with triumph. There were trölls, I knew it!

Abruptly, Þórbjörg stood up, smoothing her hand over her backside, she started for the house. Her skirt swished and billowed, as her long legs strode firmly up the walk.

I followed with somewhat subdued elation. I wanted the trölls to be real, and at the same time, I didn't. I wasn't too terribly afraid they'd catch me if only I saw them first. I could tell from the drawings of the trölls that Björssi had shown me, that their faces were extremely ugly, their bodies warty and lumpy. But many were only about the size of a medium pig with very, very short legs. I was sure I could easily outrun them any time. After all, I was always chosen to be on the relay team at school. I might not be able to outrun a giant tröll like Grýla and her ilk, but they lived near Vík, on the south side of the country.

As I entered the house, Aunty turned and gave me "that look". I knew I'd better drop the subject. She and Mother had this similarity in correcting a misbehavior; no angry words, no spanking, just what Sísí, Lilla and I called "That look". Frankly, many times I'd rather had the spanking than the guilty feeling I got from "that look."

Ólafur and Lilla had been busy. Soup-bowls and coffee cups were on the table and a couple of glasses of milk for us girls. I knew I'd get coffee later, so I thanked my uncle and took a sip.

The lively music from old Olga's harmonica drifted into the kitchen. She might be old and blind, and at times exceedingly cranky, but she could sure belt out the music! I envied her ability and tried to imitate her style when Bjössi tried to teach me. I did better playing the accordion, but wasn't very good at that either.

The music stopped, and Olga came into the kitchen scooting her feet across the floor, guided by Ólafur. Her white hair was tucked up into a green nightcap that folded over the left side of her face. The long, white tassel on the end flopped across her face as she sank heavily into her chair. Wiggling and sighing she tucked her ample skirt under her thick thighs.

"Your Grandfather will be here pretty soon to pick you up, Diddamín." Aunty was dipping up mouth-watering mutton soup as she spoke. "He'll want to load up his supplies and head home so he won't miss the out-going tide." Turning, she looked at me and asked:

"Do you have your bags ready?"

I nodded, knowing that if we missed the tide it would add hours to our travel time to Hámundarstaðir, since we'd have to skirt around the inlet instead of across it to get over to the other side. Lilla and I had been in Vopnafjörður for three weeks while Sísí had gone directly to Grandpa's farm. It was planned that Lilla and I would be with Aunty for a while, and then I would join Sísí. I was now old enough to help with the hay.

The sounds of trotting, snorting horses, jangling of harnesses, and the barking of old Snati brought us out of the house on a dead run. I leaped into Grandpa's arms as Lilla wrapped her arms around his right leg. Sísí was being hugged by Aunty and Ólafur, all of us talking and laughing at the same time. We secured the four horses to the weather-beaten wood posts, and then arm in arm went inside. Ólafur walked across the kitchen and took down several cups and saucers. Lining them up on the table, he poured coffee into each cup then sat down. Each of us reached over and helped ourselves. Aunt Þórbjörg dipped up soup for Sísí and Grandpa.

"Did the tremor do any damage at the farm, Dad?" Þórbjörg asked handing him a brimming bowl.

"No. Not at our place," he said. "The livestock in the sheepcote got a little nervous but then enjoyed the unexpected shower of hay that tumbled down from the loft." Grandpa held his beard back with his left hand as he blew on his hot soup. "I did see where snow slithered down in the clefts between the high crags further inland. We don't have anything to worry about." His eyes twinkled, as he looked at us girls. "Just a little greeting from our peculiar country." The adults chuckled at Grandpa's wit.

Aunt Þórbjörg turned and looked at me as if to say, "See, I told you so!"

Chapter 7

On My Way to Grandpa's Farm

As we came to the top of the moss and lichen-covered lava ridge, we could see the tide was way out. Grandpa's timing was perfect. He guided his horse, Blési, the lead horse, into the deep hoof-ruts carved out by many years of use. The three packhorses followed. Two of them were loaded down with 50-pound bags of flour, sugar and various other supplies grandpa had stocked up. Plus each horse carried me on one and Sísí on the other. The third horse was a young colt that carried my suitcase and a food satchel. Grandpa allowed only lightweight on the young horse while training him.

The sure-footed Icelandic horses trod down the lava-rock-riddled hill with ease, even though the two of them carried the extra weight of Sísí and me. We sat squarely in the middle, legs spread apart over the bags, our hands tightly gripping the two packsaddle pommels. The load was well balanced, and the easy gait of the horses was like sitting in a rocking chair, but gently swaying side to side instead of back and forth.

We stopped at the edge of the ocean inlet. Blési snorted and pulled toward a small, gurgling creek that tumbled down the hillside and into the shallow, salty bay.

With one easy movement, Grandpa was out of the saddle and leading his horse to the water. Digging into his pocket he pulled out a handsome cow-horn snuff holder, intricately carved, and silver adorned. Removing the ornate cap, he made a deep hollow behind his left hand by curving his forefinger and thumb, and then poured in a generous amount of snuff. Sniffing deeply, and with a loud "Ahh" he started checking the girths, harnesses and baggage, giving extra yank on the oilskin covering the flour and sugar.

I loosened the reins of Stjarna and stared across the bay. The horses were enjoying the short break and started nibbling on the sparse, pale-green, grass. Sísí's horse, Sokkur, and the colt, Töfri, were slurping noisily in the ice-cold creek. A flock of geese darted off in a flutter of feathers, while the gannets haughtily stuck their long, pointy bills into the air, flew up and then came after us, angry at being disturbed. By beating the air with our horsewhips, and yelling back at their screeching, we fought them off.

"Grandpa, why didn't you use your boat this time?" I asked. I'd thought that he preferred to use his fishing boat to travel across the bay to the village.

"The motor has been acting up. I've got it apart to clean. I'll have it ready for the next trip in." Grandpa shaded his eyes against the misty sun, dimly glimmering through low-lying clouds over the dark, distant hills.

Rubbing his grey-whiskered chin, his eyes scoured the seashore across the bay. Then chuckling, he pointed to the mouth of the inlet; the surface quivered and rippled. Sisi and I held our breath as five little brown heads popped up and large, shining black eyes inspected us with curiosity. The baby seals were totally unafraid. I guess they sensed we were not hunters. We watched as they playfully swam and dived up and down barking noisily, until older seals showed up and shooed them out to the open ocean.

"Those Harbor seals know the tide is about to turn. We'd better go across now." Grandpa swung into the stirrup of his saddle and whistled for Snati. Patting the rump of his horse, he motioned to his dog. "Come up here, old man." The stirrups skimmed the top of the sea as Grandpa urged Blési into the water that came up to the horses' knees.

Icelandic horses are small, only about 12.2 to 14.1 hands high and weigh 600 - 900 pounds. Some Polar bears are bigger than that. People in other countries often refer to them as "ponies" but they are a true Icelandic horse, having been brought to the country by Vikings in the mid-800s AD. My first ancestors arrived in 840 AD and may have brought some of them.

Icelanders are very protective of the purity of the breed, and foreign horses are not allowed into the country. If an Icelandic horse is sold and transported overseas, it is not allowed to come back.

Turning in his saddle Grandpa looked at us.

"Hold the pommels with both hands but give the horse a free rein," he said. "Our horses are quite used to this path, but the ocean floor can change with every earth tremor, even a small one like we just had, and leave pockets of holes. If Sokkur and Stjarna stop, don't urge them on. Just wait and let them decide if it's safe to go on. I'll be watching."

Sísí and I somberly nodded. I peered into the water, while my sister warily eyed me with Aunt Þórbjörg's don't-you-dare look. I grinned at her impishly and whispered:

"If you look real close Sísí, there's some kind of gruesome, greenish tail right by Sokkur's right foot!" I made a big show of squinting my eyes as I looked down.

"If there is, Sokkur would stop!" She hissed. "You can scare Lilla, but not me!"

I would have been better off paying attention to my horse. She kept swishing and lifting her tail, her rump giving out loud rumbling noises. Then Stjarna stopped, and the others kept going. Slowly I became aware that I wasn't sitting upright. I was leaning precariously to the left, my body slowly inching down until my long braids brushed the water. Just as I opened my mouth to yell, Stjarna shifted her body, my head went under and I ended up with a mouth full of salty water that went down my throat the wrong way.

"Grandpa! Stjarna's girth is loose! Íeda is drowning!" I heard Sísí shrieking at the top of her lungs. The next thing I knew Grandpa's strong arms were lifting me up and putting me onto Töfri's back. He then handed me his, reeking of tobacco, red-bandana to dry my face as I gagged and spit. I felt chastened, I should know better than to joke about the water monsters!

"What's the matter, old girl?" Grandpa ran his hand over Stjarna's flank. "Ah, gas!" Tightening the girth again, he lifted me off Töfri.

"You'll be alright now on Stjarna, Diddamín, Töfri has all he can carry." I nodded. Grandpa was very protective of his horses and took exceeding good care of them. Although Icelandic horses can carry one third of their weight he liked to wait until the colts were four to five years old before breaking them to saddle. He was very aware of the weight he put on his colts.

Halfway across the inlet the first wave rolled in, almost imperceptibly, and water was now up to the belly of our horses. Reaching the shore, they quickly scrambled up the black volcanic sand that was littered with slimy kelp and brown seaweed. Their hoofs slid as they worked their way between wet, barnacle-riddled, lava rocks until we reached the mossy bank. Following the ruts, we reached a slight hill where we dismounted.

Snati took off like an arrow shot from a bow. A riotous sound of squawks and whirring of feathers shattered the quiet countryside as a flock of rjúpa flew from the hollows of the moss-covered basalt rocks. Snati came back with a self-satisfied look on his old face. His mouth was open, long tongue flopping as he mightily shook his body. He looked like he was laughing his head off.

I had asked how old the dog was. No one could agree on his exact age, but I thought he might be as old as Grandpa. They both had grey whiskers.

Snati was a superb livestock herder. No dog, in any of the nearby farms, was as good as he was in herding the sheep during réttir - roundup - a festive fall celebration among farmers as they separated, and claimed, their sheep according to their markings. He was relentless and didn't care how far up into the mountains he had to go. Grandpa truly had bragging rights when it came to his dog, a powerfully built animal with a thick, shiny coat, mostly black in color. His four paws were brown-tipped as were his long straight ears. He had a tuft of brown on the very tip of his tail.

While Snati was lapping at a small pond, fed by a short, tumbling waterfall and the horses nibbled at grass tufts, Sísí and I sat cross-legged on the soft, grey moss while Grandpa perched on a large lava boulder. I ran my hand over a small berry-patch, but it was too early in the season. The blueberries were green, rock-hard nubs, just barely starting to grow. It will be August before I get to taste them! I sighed.

Then I saw Grandpa opening a brown burlap sack. Digging into the bag, he handed us dark, rye-bread sandwiches with thick slices of cheese and heavily smeared with butter. Pulling out a long piece of dried cod, he peeled off strips and handed them to us. Then each of us got two twist cookies as dessert. We ate contently for a while, watching the inlet fill up as the tide swept in. The silvery bodies of salmon and trout shot up into the air and dropped back into the water with soft, plopping sounds. Rings formed on the water and floated to the shores in ever widening, diminishing circles.

A seagull winged her way down and landed on a small patch of gravel, cocking her head first to one side then the other. She eyed me for a moment with her beady eyes, and then swiftly took off toward me. I could just read her tiny mind. She was after my cookies! I jumped up and shooed her away amid the screaming of other greedy gulls that had now gathered to grab their share. One headed for Sísí and I yelled;

"Get her Sísí, get her!"

"How do you know it's a 'her'?" Grandpa roared with laughter as he too was fighting off the crazy birds.

"Well, this bird just looked smaller than the others and just *looked* like a 'lady-bird,' but she sure didn't act like one!" I huffed, out of breath.

As we gathered up what food was left over, a thick band of fog was rolling in from the mouth of the fjord. We heard the motors of a couple of fishing boats start up and watched as they headed toward Vopnafjörður harbor.

"Well," Grandpa drawled, "looks like we got across just in time. From the looks of that fog, we may be in for a soupy time. We'd better get a move on."

After washing down our food from the little waterfall, we remounted. With Blési leading, we continued in the hoof-ruts that were so deep in places that grandpa's feet were literally dragging on the ground. He lifted his feet and spread them out wide as he came to higher mounds of moss and grass-covered rocks. My mare, Stjarna, was at the end of the 'caravan'.

The days were getting longer and we would have no real darkness from now until fall. The nights would get lighter and lighter until the sun would dangle on the horizon all night. Now, only a dusky, grey sky gave an eerie look to the black, craggy cliffs. A small farmstead sat far back in the hills, barely discernable in the gravelly background. Streams wandered and gurgled down in small waterfalls then disappeared into gravel beds. The countryside was bleak and sparse. Meager grass tufts were sprinkled with small patches of purple wild flowers, which somehow were able to find roots between the moss and lichen. The huge waves of white fog were now wallowing in like a slow-moving avalanche.

Chapter 8

The Fog

Grandpa held his right hand up, indicating we should stop. He then took a rope from his saddlebag and rode in front of Sokkur. Tying the rope to the pommel in front of Sísí he then proceeded to tie Töfri. Stjarna was next. He guided Blési to the back holding the rope loosely in his hand as he motioned to my sister.

"Sísí, Sokkur will now lead," he said. "The fog may get so thick we'll not be able to see one another. I want to be sure we don't get separated." Sísí nodded.

Well, for once I was very happy to be in the middle. I thought the oozing, slithery fog in Vopnafjörður was absolutely the creepiest thing. It always seemed to me that the whole countryside became a completely different world, filled with ghostly cities and 'hidden people' constantly moving and changing shapes At the same time I was fascinated by the strangeness of the grey-white, rolling mist that never looked the same.

Our sure-footed horses plodded along, staying in the deep path. They didn't hesitate or stumble, even when the fog caught up with us and the rut totally disappeared from sight. In no time, it was as if we'd been covered with a huge, silver-grey downy duvet. The swirling damp fog was tangible, filling my mouth and nose. I felt I could take a handful and wad it up like a snowball. I could no longer see Sísí, and Töfri was a moving grey blur. I turned and looked behind me. Grandpa was a hunched-down shadowy shroud, rocking side to side.

* * *

Then came the welcoming sounds of hoofs clomping on the wooden bridge that spanned a small glacial-fed creek which swiftly rushed by Hámundarstaðir.

Suddenly, there was a small rift in the fog, as if someone had flung back gauzy curtains. A slight wind had come up, and slowly the fog dissipated in twists, swirls and spirals. The path widened, flattened and became more visible.

"We are here, we made it!" Sísí yelled eagerly.

She had spotted the open gate with the metal arch proclaimin 'HÁMUNDARSTAÐIR' etched in bold letters. The loaded-down horses picked up their pace and trotted up to the front door as it was flung open by Björssi, Grandma Sigríður and Grand-amma following close at his heels.

Grandpa's farmhouse was a complex of three wood gable fronts, built side-by-side and divided by two short walls of rock and turf. The roof and each end of the gables was covered with turf that grew thick, green grass where we, constantly, had to chase off the sheep. This type of farmhouse was called burstabær (gable farm). In the middle gable was the main entrance to the hall, the passageway to the kitchen, and the stairs to Grandpa's attic room.

The left-side wall of the dark, hard-packed dirt floor was finished with rough, wooden boards. Several wood pegs were placed at various heights for men's, women's, and children's coats. Also there were pegs for the horsewhips everyone owned; light-weight, heavy-weight, short, long. Some plain and some very elegantly silver adorned, handsomely carved with initials of the owner. An assortment of bridles were hung on heavy, higher-up pegs. The right side of the hall had a wall of various size stone and daubed with solidly packed dirt, and a door leading to the cow-house, very convenient for milking in the winter.

A narrow dung-trough went across the entire width and to the opposite wall. About a foot up this wall was a two-foot square opening with a hinged door. On the other side was a huge hole where Bjössi pitched the manure, which in time seeped and disappeared in the porous volcanic ground.

This was also the bathroom when it was too cold to go outside to the outhouse. When I had to squat over the dung-trough to use the 'facility,' I had to be sure to hold a cow's tail or I'd get a whopping of a slap!

Just outside the front door was the hitching rock where we, or guests, would tie the horses' reins. A weathervane sat on top of the central gable. The small outhouse nearby was also covered with turf, except for the front where the wood door with the half-moon was.

Bjössi lifted Sísí off the packsaddle as Grandpa dismounted and came to Stjarna. Swinging me down and holding me in his arms as if I were a baby, he handed me to Grandma, who promptly started kissing and hugging me. Sísí stood by, grinning ear to ear. I could tell by the gleeful look on her face that she was just dying to tell Grandma how she'd saved my life. She'd probably tell that I was teasing her about the monster-worm. I glanced at her sideways. She looked like she'd swallowed the whole bird. Hmm, how can I stop her? I'd have to come up with something mighty quick!

"It's wonderful to see you, Diddamín!" Grand-Amma got up from her rocking chair shooing the plump black cat off her lap. Grýla yowled and took off, swishing her tail with displeasure, then ran over and rubbed against my ankles as Grand-Amma gave me a tight hug. With her arm resting on my shoulder, she turned to Sísí.

"Pour us some coffee, my love, and tell me all about Þórbjörg, and the trip," she said. "I was really concerned when the fog rolled in so quickly." Grand-Amma sat back down with a deep sigh. She was rather heavy set and quickly got short of breath.

I helped Sísí get the cups and saucers off the wood shelf. We settled ourselves in the kitchen where boiling coffee and soup blended in a delicious aroma, permeating the air. My stomach growled so loud that Grandma Sigríður exclaimed, "Are you starving? Didn't that man feed you?" She glared at Grandpa who was coming in the door, slapping and rubbing his cold hands together.

"Oh yes, Grandma. He fed us!" Sísí and I spoke up at the same time.

"It just smells so good in here that my stomach got greedy!" I jumped up and grabbed Grandma around her neck. "I'm so very happy to be here. I liked it at Auntie's house too, but I really missed all of you and missed doing things with Sísí." I sneaked a look at her. Maybe she'd go easy on me!

"Oh, it'll be fun to have you here. We'll go egg hunting and berry-picking, milking old Rauða...," she said, then stopped and gave me a big grin. Was my sister being her nice self, or was there a wicked gleam in her eye as she mentioned the milking? I was sure that Grandpa's "Old Rauða" was the meanest tempered cow in all of Iceland!

Íeda Jónasdóttir Herman

Chapter 9

Gamla Rauða (Old Red)

As Sísí and I entered the cow-house, the chickens, and especially the threatening, vicious, rooster, cackled and fussed.

Each time I stuck my hand into a nest to gather eggs he'd spread out his red-gold wings, screech, and glare at me with his glittering, tiger-yellow eyes. One of these days, Grandma will get tired you attacking her and us. She'll wring your scrawny neck and you'll end up in the stew-pot, I thought to myself, glaring back, then followed Sisi as she went to the cow-stall.

She carried the milk-bucket in her right hand while holding onto me with her left. I tiptoed alongside her, carefully sidestepping Rauða's droppings. Clutching a three-legged wooden milk-stool with both hands, I tried not to breathe the potent dung smell.

"Now hold tight onto Rauða's tail, don't let her whack me!" Sísí swept a squawking chicken off another cow's back and took the stool out of my hands, then stomped ahead of me to Rauða's stall.

Sisi detested milking the cows, detested going into the reeking stall, and detested Rauða, who either slapped you with her gross tail or sent gross, slimy yuck with her long tongue. The nasty tempered cow would kick your leg, or milk-bucket at every opportunity, and she was forever butting her horns into the wall where she had dug out a huge hole. I thought for sure that one day she'd gore an opening right through the thick, dirt wall.

Rauða was one crabby old cow.

"Why don't you tie the tail to her leg?" I grumbled. "That's what Grandma does." I didn't like this chore either.

Sisi glared at me. "No, just hold the tail!"

I did my best. My arms flew side to side as the cow tried to loosen my grip. I gritted my teeth and held on; *I would've tied the yucky thing!*

Sísí did a good job. The spurts of milk made pinging sounds as they hit the inside of the tin pail, the milky froth piling up. Rauða was a mean-spirited cow but she gave lots of good milk, with very thick cream. Her udder was full and tight with milk and must have been quite uncomfortable; she seemed rather subdued for a change. I should have been suspicious.

After the milking, Sísí stood up and placed the pail in the corner by the door. I let go of the tail and Rauða, predictably, relieved of the weight on her udder, promptly kicked back and sent the stool flying into the side of Freyja, the heifer in the next stall. The ensuing out-of-control bedlam that followed was stupefying; cows bellowing - chickens loudly squawking - Sísí and I wildly screaming and jumping, trying to get out of the way of madly flailing tails. There wasn't a whole lot of room for us to duck.

"Stupid, dumb cow!" I yelled as I got swatted across the back.

"What in heavens name is going on?" Grandma Sigríður came running into the cow-house.

"Old Rauða got mad at me for holding her tail." I was steamed.

"Well, she's used to her tail being tied, try *that* the next time." Grandma shook her head as she picked up the milk bucket and went to the kitchen. Glancing at Sísí I tried to give her the Aunty Þórbjörg's " I told you so" look. It didn't do me any good. My sister completely ignored me.

We followed grandma into the kitchen where she poured the

milk into the two-spout separator. Grand-Amma, was sitting on a stool, her left hand on the handle ready to crank the machine. Pretty soon, the thick cream came out of one spout while thinner milk gushed out of the other. Grandma poured the cream into a wooden churn. Sísí and I took turns in sloshing the butter-paddle up and down, until we heard the solid mass of butter plopping in the bottom. Grandma reached down into the churn, took out the big blob of butter and salted it.

The mouth-watering aroma of baking bread permeated the kitchen, along with the constantly-cooking mutton soup that cooked away all day. Grand-Amma pulled the bread out of the oven and set it beside the always-brewing coffeepot. I sniffed deeply, devouring the delicious bouquet mix.

Slicing the hot bread, Grandma Sigríður put on a thick slab of butter before handing us each a slice. The melting butter ran between our fingers and we licked as fast as we could, Sísí ever-so-daintily. I slurped mine "'cause it was slurpy-licking good!"

Grandma picked up the pail containing the thinner [skimmed] milk, and walked over to the storage area of the kitchen and poured the milk into a short wood tub. Next to it sat the pickled herring, pickled whale blubber and the singed-and-pickled sheep heads, with eyeballs intact, all preserved and stored in wooden barrels. There was also a barrel of pickled ram testicles. We girls gagged at the thought and refused to eat it. There also was a barrel-pickled blood-pudding.

From a rack above the barrels hung a side of smoked mutton and dried cod, which we liked very much and could nibble on all day! There was also fermented shark, though not our favorite food.

Grandma added a small clump of skyr [yogurt] from a previous batch and dumped it into the skimmed-milk tub. This clump would start the 'setting' process for a new batch. She would then save a handful from this batch to be added to the next. This method of making skyr started with the Vikings. For centuries, a small batch has always been saved to continue the fermenting process.

The next day we would have more of the yummy skyr. We ate the scrumptious yogurt for breakfast, with cream and sugar sprinkled on top. Later in the summer, we would top it with blueberries when the berries were ripe.

Chapter 10

Haying Time

"I'll have lunch ready in a little while. Both of you will need to go out to the field and take the food to your grandpa and the workers." Grandma said as she turned to me. "Diddamín, Sokkur and Stjarna are just outside the fence. Go and get them while Sísí helps me to finish up here."

Grand-Amma, who had been watching Grandma as she bustled about, arose from her chair with a deep sigh and followed me out of the kitchen.

"I guess you both are riding bareback as usual?" She asked in somewhat disapproving tone. "The way you two gallivant on those horses isn't very lady-like." Shaking her head, she reaching a blue-veined hand to one of the higher pegs and took down two bridles.

I grinned as I took the harnesses out of her hands. Sísí and I knew that Grand-Amma thought the only way for ladies to ride a horse was side-saddle, in a culottes-style split skirt.

"Thanks, Grand-Amma. You are right; Sísí and I won't be bothering with saddles." I gave her a quick peck on the cheek and darted out the door.

I jogged across the lumpy field. The bridles clunked on my shoulder as I leaped between moss-covered lava rocks. At the noise, Stjarna and Sokkur lifted their heads from nibbling the meager, pale-green tufts of grass. Neighing and snorting they ambled toward me.

Töfri came running and nuzzled against me. I liked him. He

was growing up to be very special. He had a shiny, silver-grey coat and coal-black mane and tail. His eyes were large, bright and intelligent. I rubbed behind his left ear. He seemed to sense my affection and whinnied softly.

"Sorry, Boy. You stay put." I patted his black, velvety-soft nose.

Stjarna and Sokkur trotted up as I rattled the reins. I got the bit in their mouths, gave Töfri a couple of sugar cubes then swatted him on the rump and watched as he scampered away.

Stjarna [Star] was a reliable, grey mare, with a long, white mane and tail. Sokkur [Socks] was glistening-black, with a white, narrow stripe from his eyes down to his nostrils, and white 'socks' on all four feet. They all held their head proudly, a sure sign of loved and well-tended horses.

Stepping up on top of one of the rocks, I jumped on Stjarna's back, and holding Sokkur's rein, we went at a gallop back to the farmhouse.

Grand-Amma, Grandma and Sísí were all outside waiting. I didn't dismount since the food was all packed and ready. My sister put her left foot on the hitching-rock, swung her right foot over Sokkur's back and wiggled a bit, as she settled herself. Each of us had food satchels and milk pails in front of us. We waved as we headed for the valley where Grandpa, uncle Björsi, and their summer help, Helgi, Guðrún, and Dísa were cutting and drying hay.

Grass grew sparsely around the farm and Grandpa had to go way up into the foothills of the mountains to find enough to cut, and store away for the winter.

We went at an easy canter past the stable, down the lane, and over the bridge. As soon as we crossed the bridge the horses went swiftly into rack, and then into flying pace, a five-gait that's unique to Icelandic horses. Björsi liked to show off the smooth gait by carrying a glass of water and riding at break-neck speed on his horse, Thunder, not spilling a single drop.

Sokkur and Stjarna kept up the galloping run across the outer field, until we reached the start of the foothills. We heard the whinnying of Blési before seeing him. Our horses neighed back. Biting at their bits, they eagerly plunged up the hill that led to an incredible volcanic cliff formation pointing to the sky with mystic shapes and deep crevasses. If that isn't the perfect place for trölls, I don't know what is, I thought to myself. Suddenly, a couple of ptarmigans scrambled away from the hooves of Stjarna, startling me but not my calm horse.

"Hey Sísí, you know there are trölls living up there, don't you?" My hands were gripping the reins. The mare sensed my tension. She shook her head and grunted, both in displeasure with me and exertion with going uphill.

Sísí turned, dark brows knit tightly over the bridge of her nose. "Stop it, Íeda. Iceland is weird, and weird things happen, but there are NO TRÖLLS!"

She shouted the last words. Why is she shouting? I wondered. And how did she get to be so grown up and sound like Aunty? She's is just eleven years old, and I'm nine and a half. I stared at the high crags where few, long fingers of wispy fog were curling over the edges. The cool sun was playing hide and seek in fluffy, cottony clouds, sending eerie, grey shadows stealthily moving across the mountain.

I turned and looked down toward the ocean. Hámundarstaðir was hard to see unless you knew where to look; the turf roof blended with the ground. The farm looked like a toy house in the distance, sitting precipitously at the very edge on the cliff that skirted the long fjord.

The horses clambered over the last hill, and there were the workers.

Grandpa's scythe was swinging up and down, Helgi was a few feet behind him and Bjössi a few feet behind Helgi. Each man had a firm grip on the two knobby handles on the long pole, swinging their scythes in perfect rhythm; *up-down-swish-up-down-swish...* the curve of the sharp blades smoothly cutting the grass. The two women followed behind raking the newly cut, green leaves into rows of long, narrow piles. Four bales of hay were tied up and ready to be taken to the farm.

"Lunch time!" Sísí and I hollered unnecessarily as the workers were already laying down their tools. The rare sun had made all of them work up a sweat, their lopi sweaters were piled up on a large lava rock.

The men pulled out their fancy tobacco-horns. Grandpa's was by far the most ornate. He and Bjössi poured snuff on the back of their left hand while Helgi poured his on the back of his right hand. Snuffing mightily, each sat down on a moss-covered rock.

Guðrún handed the bags to Dísa who started passing the food around. The two women, both in their twenties, were as different as night and day. Blond-haired Guðrún was short and slim with sky-blue twinkled eyes. Merry, easy-going and given to teasing, she and Bjössi got along extremely well. She was also a whirlwind of a worker that Grandpa really appreciated. Dísa had red hair and a temper to go with it. Striking, almost-green eyes, tall and graceful, she also pulled no punches when it came to work.

Helgi was a quiet, thirty-something, brown-haired, square-built man, well known for his strength. He was an undefeated arm-wrestler in the area. Even though there was such an age difference, he and Bjössi complemented each other. Eighteen year-old Bjössi was outgoing in nature, very popular with the young folks as he played his accordion at many country-dances in the village.

After lunch was finished, we put everything away and went back to work. We hustled for several hours, the men cutting grass steadily, occasionally stopping to sharpen their scythes. They'd pull out a pumice stone from their back pocket, spit on the scythe blades, then swish the stone back and forth, starting at the pole and following the curve of the blade to the end of the point. Periodically they'd check the blade with a thumb until satisfied with its sharpness.

Guðrún and Dísa followed, raking and turning the rows of grass, it smelled faintly of thyme and crowberry leaves. Sísí and I did our best to keep up. My sister was getting pretty good. She seemed to be able to just go ahead and work, whereas I tended to stop and breathe the aroma of the grass, look around, and frequently inspect the odd-looking, black lava cliff.

I leaned on my rake and wiped the sweat off my face with the back of my hand, staring for a minute at the rocky crags then went back to raking. After a while, I looked where we had been working. None of the rows were straight for any length. Several outcrops of rocks were scattered about and we had to work around them. I hope we aren't disturbing the 'Hidden Folks' that live in those rocks, I thought. At least we aren't moving any of them like some farmers have done and grief came upon them and their household!

Lost in my daydreaming I accidentally dropped my rake. It clattered noisily against one of the boulders. Shivering and mumbling an apology, I started raking like one possessed! Sísí turned at the noise.

"Wow, you sure got pumped all of a sudden!" She grinned. She sure has a way of reading my mind; I glared at her as I chewed on my bottom lip. Turning away from my sister, I concentrated on my raking.

The dangling sun in the northern sky was hidden in the crimson-streaked clouds that brushed the tips of the cliffs. To the east, the clouds on the horizon touched the mouth of the fjord. Sky and sea were turning dark-grey, and, as so often in the fjords, it was hard to tell where one started and the other ended.

The wind was picking up and it was getting chilly. We put our lopi sweaters back on and prepared to quit for the day and head back to the farm.

Grandpa got one of the horses and fastened a packsaddle on its back. He hoisted one of the bales of hay and hooked it on the right side peg. Then he motioned for me to do my job. I knew what to do, bending over I backed my butt up against the flank of the horse and under the bale, holding it up while Grandpa went around and lifted another bale onto the left side peg. Bjössi put a packsaddle on another horse and lifted up a bale of hay. Sísí held it up in the same manner as I had for Grandpa as the other bale was put into place.

Helgi, Guðrún, and Dísa got the rest of our horses and our "caravan" started for home.

I could never figure out how Grandpa could get those bales so perfectly balanced. He had no scales to weigh them.

Grandpa was a very smart man!

Chapter 11

Eider Bird Egg-Hunting

Sitting on the soft, grey, moss-covered volcanic cliff, Sísí and I dangled our legs over the edge, watching the white-crested ocean waves roll in. Two screeching seagulls circled, then dove at our heads. They flew off as we stood up, waving our hands, shooing them away.

We could feel the shaking of the ground as powerful ocean waves crashed against the rocks, and sent up columns of, shooting, ocean spray into the air. Fine, salty mist clung to our wooly caps and moistened our faces. Not a hint of fog anywhere for a change. Tall, white waterfalls cascaded down Smjörfell Mountain in the distance. The rivers meandered in curvy ribbons down the valley and emptied into the fjord. The ice-blue sky was filled with big bales of white, cottony clouds that sailed along in the cool, brisk, steady breeze.

Tucking our hair tighter under our lopi-knit caps, we scanned the eider ducks flying about, then coming down and waddling to a nest, we hoped, among the rocks on the damp lava sand.

"There are hundreds of ducks. We should be able to get tons of eggs and down!" I whispered, although we were a good twenty feet above the ocean beach. The insane noise of the gulls and krias, and the pounding of the sea, would have made it virtually impossible for the ducks to hear me.

"Some of them went to the moss patch behind the big boulder where that seal is, he'll leave when he sees us come down. Let's go." Sísí said as she started scrambling like a fly down the, almost-sheer, rock wall. I followed close behind. With tiny toeholds and small ledges for our fingers to grip, we crept down, causing loose shale and lava rocks to roll. The clatter disturbed some haughty-gaudy puffins that pompously waddled away.

We had two flour sacks tied to our waist; one for the Down and one for the eggs. I looked forward to eating those scrumptious eggs. They tasted stronger than chicken eggs and were about three times as big, with huge, reddish-yellow yolk.

The last few feet were loose pebbles and sand. We skidded down on our bottoms until we reached the beach. Catching our breath for a moment, we sat still as two groups of grey geese spanned their wings wide, flapped and squawked raucously, and then went at each other. I saw what they were fighting over; a large, dead trout lay on the ground halfway between the two. They separated and flew off as we got up and started to walk toward them. I was glad it wasn't gannets, they would have attacked us in a heartbeat' with their saber-like pointy beaks.

Sísí was right. The seal belly-flopped off the rock, then, awkwardly, flip-flopped on the pebbly beach to the ocean and smoothly swam away.

We found some nests and gathered two dozen eggs, always leaving one or two in the down-filled nest to hatch, since Eider ducks rarely lay more than five eggs. We divided our eggs in two bags and carefully tucked some down all around them, then filled the other bags with the soft, downy, feathers.

"Grandma will be happy to know there are so many nests here." Sisi said, as she tightened the string on her sack and fastened it back to her waist. "She was wanting to make more bed-pillows. If it doesn't rain tomorrow, we'll have to get a group of us together and come back." She started to walk back toward the cliff.

"Wait a minute, Sísí. Let's wade for a while." I said. "Look, there is a small cave over there! The ocean is so clear, I see some pretty neat seashells on the bottom." I sat down on a rock and started to take off my shoes, then jumped up howling:

"Oh gross! A fulmar has spit his yellow gook here. The rock smells of rotten fish!"

Sísí was doubled over with laughter as she unfastened her bags. Turning, she pointed to where we had clawed our way down.

"There are a lot of them nesting in the hollows of the sea-cliff; we're lucky we didn't touch their mess. We'd be stinking to high heaven for days!" She gave an exaggerated shudder.

Taking off our shoes and socks we tiptoed among the shells and pebbles. I stuck my foot into the pool.

"Wow, the water is ice-cold" I yelped, yanking my foot back, shivering.

Looking down I saw little fish darting about. Large, silvery, trout swam gracefully in the pond-like water in the shallow cave that had been carved out by the unceasing surging of the ocean waves.

Hollering "EE-OW" at the top of our lungs, we waded in the freezing sea waves hopping backward as a wave would roll in and slosh white froth up our legs. The hems on our skirts were getting soaked; it was time for us to go home.

We fastened our bags to our waists and headed back up. As Sísí and I clambered up on all fours, the sandy shale caused our feet to slide one foot back for every two feet upward. Our soggy sheepskin shoes and wool socks were soon caked with powdery, black volcanic sand.

Although the wind was nippy, we had beads of sweat on our foreheads by the time we reached the top. We jammed our hats tighter on our heads. The ends of our lopi-scarfs whipped across our shoulders and flapped behind us as we, puffing and breathing hard, walked and skipped back to the farmhouse.

This had been a wonderful day. I looked at Sísí and grinned. I hadn't said anything about the trölls, the awful Grýla, and Leppalúður (well, actually that's really a Christmas thing, I'll wait!) And I hadn't breathed a *word* about the 'Hidden Folks' who were in abundance in this region.

For a change, I'd been VERY good!

Chapter 12

Sísí and I go Berry Picking

"The blueberries should be ripe about now, and I'd like to have some to make jam, and top our skyr," Grandma said as she walked into the kitchen. "How about you two go and pick some, and don't bother with picking any crowberries." Reaching under the bench, she pulled out two tin buckets. Each had a folded, white flour sack. "The weather looks good and your grandfather and Björssi have already taken the boat over to Vopnafjörður. Dísa and Guðrún are hoeing the garden and cutting the Rabarbarinn [Rhubarb]," she continued as she handed us two bulging lunch satchels.

"We love to go berry picking!" Both of us cried enthusiastically, jumping up from our stools. We smiled gleefully at each other at the same thought: Riding into the valley the berry hunting and picking would take most of the day. We'd be gone at milking time and wouldn't have to put up with mean Rauða!

"Shall we go back to the foothills where we are haying?" Sísí asked casually, as she reached around doorpost and got couple of rope-bridles.

"The cows meandered over that way, look for them and bring them back with you after you've filled your buckets." Grandma said grinning. She knew exactly what we'd been thinking! I squirmed, a guilty blush warming my cheeks. Sísí turned with a shrug, wrinkling her nose.

"We'll do that Grandma." She said. Slinging one halter over

her shoulder and handing me the other one, Sísí reached down and picked up her pail and satchel as I picked up mine. We kissed Grandma on the cheek, then went out the door and headed for the field. We waved to Dísa and Guðrún. They had paused working to wipe the sweat off their foreheads with white handkerchiefs. Leaning on the handles of their hoes, they waved back.

Snati and Goldie got to their feet, stretching. The dainty Goldie lifted up her right paw, grooming it with long strokes by her tongue. Snati sat up, his dark-brown eyes glittering as he cocked his head.

"Yes you may go with us." I said patting his head. His body quivered with excitement. He was probably ten years older than Goldie, but still acted and worked like a much younger dog, and he was *ten* times smarter than she!

Sísí whistled for the horses as we sauntered past the sheepcote. The horses were in the outer field and came trotting toward us. As usual, I got Stjarna while Sísí put the bridle on Sokkur. We didn't use saddles unless we were visiting a neighboring farm, or on a trip to the village of Vopnafjörður or north to Bakkafjörður.

After a brisk, one-hour ride, we got close to where we'd been haying. The fearsome, grotesquely shaped lava rock wall loomed forebodingly before us. I would never be able to understand how Sísí could be so calm, almost serene, in these eerie surroundings. I loved my rugged, bleak country, full of mysteries and adventure but I also saw ghosts and gremlins in every crack and crevasse!

We went past piles of blue-grey lava chunks spaced few meters apart. Travelers from centuries ago had stacked up these landmarks - tall ones and squatty ones - as guideposts.

Dotting the valley were towering, skinny, lava-formed pillars with grey-black trunks. Their tops were covered with the grey velvety moss that was everywhere. Small, white and purple flowers were somehow able to grab roots in non-existing soil.

After another hour of riding farther into the ravine, we spotted the cows ambling away, munching at the meager grass. A tall waterfall cascaded down the craggy, basalt-formed hill, and the wide, shallow river meandered our way. One cow was standing in mid-stream slurping away. This was a good place to stop. We led the horses down for a drink then tethered them and went to look for berry-patches. Both dogs lapped the water then scampered off to chase birds.

"Kónguló, kónguló, vísaðu mér á berjamó," [Spider, spider show me the berry-land] we chanted as we searched for ripe, juicy blueberries. We believed the old folks' stories; the spiders always led the way to the best berry-spots, and we were very careful not to squash those long-legged, helpful creatures.

Sure enough, we came upon a nice area thick with berries. It was getting close to lunch- time so we decided to eat before we started picking the fruit. Grandma had fixed enough for a small army; strips of dried cod, slices of smoked mutton, and twist-cookies. We drank fresh water from the river and then started gathering the berries. At first, I could hear them clunk into our pails, but as they accumulated, the only sound was a soft *plop*. The narrow valley was quiet. Every now and then, a ptarmigan would cluck and dart out from under a small bush, wings whirring. The horses occasionally snorted softly, and the cows chewed contently. The air was calm. A faint, salty, smell from the ocean mingled with thyme and berries. A few fluffy clouds wandered across the sharp-blue sky.

Sísí had crawled up the hillside and was furiously picking away, her left hand bending down the berry-bush, while her right hand busily picked off the berries. My bucket was over half-full, but the way she was going, I was sure she had hers almost full. I sat back on my heels and glanced at the craggy mountain. Then did a double take! Thick fog was gathering on top and oozing down the slopes!

"Sísí, look." I stood up, but she kept going. I raised my voice.

"Sísí look at the mountain." Rubbing her berry-stained hands on the moss, she got up slowly.

"I've my pail full. What about the mountain?" Then turning her head, she followed where I was pointing. "Oh no," she whispered.

"Maybe it'll move north." I said. We watched and gauged the move of the fog. Looking at each other, we wordlessly agreed it was coming our way, and by the looks of it, we were in for 'a soupy one' as Grandpa would say. Putting a pail into each flour sack, we tied the top tight to keep the berries from falling out.

Getting back on our horses, we yelled at the dogs to start the cows moving. Old Rauða mooed in protest then reluctantly led the way. The bell on her neck clanged as she started to walk in the hoof-path. Freyja didn't want to move, but Snati knew what to do; yipping from side to side he threatening to nip her legs. The heifer decided to fall in line with Rauða. The third cow, Hilda, followed. Cow-poke-slowly the parade started.

Sísí kept Sokkur close behind Hilda. I followed on Stjarna and kept twisting to look back, keeping an eye on the fog as it swirled down the crags. I, of course, was expecting to see one or more, of the 'Hidden Folks' that materialized in any good, proper fog.

Icy fingers were already playing up and down my spine when I heard an awful sound; *baagh, baagh, baagh*!

My blood ran cold and the hair on the back of my neck curled up!

With my heart thumping a mile a minute I whacked Stjarna

on the rump, moving her out of the rut and up on the bank. Catching up with Sísí I poked her arm with my horsewhip. She looked at me startled.

"What's the matter with you?" She asked, a little irritated. "The fog is still behind us, I think we'll beat it if we can get these cows to move a little faster!"

"No Sísí listen. Can't you hear it?" I asked.

Sísí stopped her horse and cocked her head just as another *baagh, baagh, baagh* resounded in the cliffs.

"It doesn't sound scary. I can't quite make it out. Wait. Look at that sheep up there, by that boulder." Sisi pointed. "She's just standing there *'baaing'*. The other ones around her are eating. Something isn't quite right." She squinted her eyes intently at the sheep.

For a moment, I stared at the ground by the boulder, then kind of recognized the sound and said to my sister.

"I bet her lamb fell into a hole and is crying down in there. That's what makes it sound so weird." I turned Stjarna and had her take a few steps toward the hillside and the sheep, she watched me, but didn't move. Then I heard the sound again *'baagh,'* and now I could tell that it was a lamb in distress. My fears were replaced with anxiety.

"Come on Sísí, we've got to get the lamb out or it'll die."

"Let's hurry then! The dogs will get the cows home, and if we get caught in the fog our horses will take us to the farm."

Quickly, Sisi turned Sokkur out of the rut and joined me on top of the bank. We went across the river and up the gravelly side of the mountain toward the large rock. The ewe warily eyed us as she backed away a few steps, and then stopped.

When we came around the boulder, we could see an opening in the ground where the yammering was coming from. As we dismounted, I looked with unease at the thick fog that had now drifted into the bottom of the valley, slowly obliterating everything in its path.

We got down on our stomachs and looked into the narrow chasm. The young lamb had left numerous marks where it had tried, in a futile attempt, to climb out. From the way it was moving around, it didn't look to have any broken limbs, but was exceedingly nervous.

"It's too deep to jump into." Sisi said as she sat back on her haunches and stared sadly at the pathetic little ewe.

"We could slide down, but we wouldn't be able to get out of there. The walls are extremely smooth. There are hardly any toeholds."

We sat for a moment contemplating our dilemma. The lamb cried piteously. From the droppings in the hole, I surmised that the lamb had been there overnight and was very hungry.

"Well, tell you what, I'm taking the bridle off of Stjarna. She won't leave," I said handing the harness to Sisi. "I'll go down, and you hand me the rope. I'll catch the lamb and strap it down then lift it up to you. Since I'm littler than you, it'll be easier for you to pull me up than for me to pull you."

Sisi gnawed her bottom lip, looking dubious. "Are you sure we should do this, Íedamin?"

"We've been in volcanic crevasses before, Sisi. No-one will be able to get here in time to save the lamb; it'll starve to death." A shudder ran down my sister's back, biting her quivering lower lip she nodded. I slid down into the hole as Sisi dropped the harness after me holding the loop end tightly in her hands.

The lamb frantically tried scramble away as I grabbed it, but I desperately held on. Wrapping my arms around it, I held the weakly-kicking feet and worked the rope around the white, wooly body. I saw the two VV cuts in the left ear, Grandpa's mark. Holding tight, I lifted the small lamb to Sisi, who was on her stomach, her hands reaching down.

"Got her," she exulted, working the small ewe from the bridle. Then I heard a soft, "Oh, she headed straight for mamma." Sisi's head came back in view. She was giggling. "Her stubby tail is a blur, she's wagging it so fast. She must have been absolutely starving. She's suckling like there's no tomorrow!"

I was happy to hear that, but I was more than ready to get out of this tröll-hole.

"Here it comes, I have my feet braced against a rock." Sisi said as the rope slithered down. I held on to the loop of the harness and pulled myself up hand-over-hand as Sisi, grunting loudly, pulled and held on.

We sat on the rim of the fissure for a moment catching our breath, watching the ewe and her lamb. We were grinning from ear to ear as we clapped our hands in joy.

We just barely beat the fog. By the time I'd put the bridle back on Stjarna, the grey, soggy mist wrapped around us. We remembered the admonition from the family:

"If you're ever caught in a fog, loosen your hold on the reins and let the horses take over; they'll know the way." They sure enough did!

This was the last time we sisters were together at Vopnafjörður. For the next four years, I traveled by myself.

Chapter 13

Vopnafjörður

1935

The two corrugated sheds where I had tried to get Lilla to jump, were askew from the earthquake last year, but still standing. I could still jump from one to the other!

I ran ahead of Aunty and Ólafur and entered the house. A low moaning-groan greeted me. I skidded to a stop, my heart thumping wildly. Then the moaning faded to a grunt, and I heard a soft voice.

"I'm sorry, just one more bandage and I'll be through." A woman said gently.

A man's gruff voice said something. I didn't understand the words, but I understood the groaning. I assumed it must be the Norwegian patient. He must be hurting bad! My heart stopped pounding as I realized what the moaning was. I turned as Aunty dropped the box on the table and went into the sickroom.

Although I didn't speak Norwegian, I'd been around sailor-fishermen often enough to recognize the language. I could hear Aunty speaking, sounded to me like she'd asked a question. The man's voice answered in a loud voice that, I thought, sounded belligerent. She returned shortly, with a wide grin on her face.

"Hans wants to get up and walk around!" she, gleefully, told Ólafur. "He is getting much better."

"He sure groaned a lot for someone who's getting better. He scared the wits out of me!" I said looking around the room, still feeling a little freaked out.

A tall, rawboned, very capable-looking woman came into the kitchen. Her abundant, orange-red, hair stuck out in all directions. It reminded me of Halldór's hair, the big man down at the warehouse.

"Halló there, and you must be the visitor from Reykjavik." Cocking her head, she measured me up from my shoes to the top of my head with her piercing green eyes.

"You're one spunky girl, aren't you? I'm Sigga." She stuck out her right hand and I stuck out mine. Her, very large, calloused hand totally made mine disappear. I winced a bit as she gave a hearty squeeze. We shook hands like two adults. She didn't call me a little one, not a little girl, but spunky. I liked the sound of it; it wasn't wimpy.

"I'm pleased to meet you. My name is Íeda." I said politely as I'd been taught. "Þórbjörg is my aunt and Ólafur is my uncle." I added primly.

"Íeda. That's an unusual name. I like it." Sigga smiled broadly.

"I don't like my name at all!" I grumbled. My dark eyebrows were pulled together in a tight knot. "Some say its Ýta, others say Íta, another Ída, still another Æda. No matter what it is, the kids at school like to make fun of it and rhyme it with bad words." I frowned, gnawing the inside of my mouth. "Grandpa said I was supposed to be named after Aunt Þórbjörg; he said my name was 'outlandish'. He calls me Didda or Diddamín. No one ever heard of my *real* name, whatever it is." I stared at the floor. My eyes felt hot. I'm not going to be a cry-baby! Grandpa always said that Viking children never cried; they howled, screamed, bellowed - but did not cry! I clenched my jaw and rubbed the floor with my toe.

"Your name must be hidden" Sigga mused, rubbing her left

thumb across her lower lip.

Auntie's chair scraped loudly on the floor as she shoved away from the table, clearing her throat.

"What?" Startled, I lifted my head and looked into Sigga's face. She had her head cocked, her left eye scrunched shut, looking first at Auntie, and then at me. Leaning close, her wild hair shook like birds shaking bush-leaves as she lowered her voice;

"No one has heard of your name, right?" She asked

I nodded. "That's right."

"No one seems to spell it correctly, right?" Her nose was just inches away from mine.

Puzzled, I nodded again. Auntie cleared her throat again, this time quite loudly.

"So you're not named after anyone in the family?"

Pursing my lips, I shook my head vigorously.

Sigga stared Auntie right in the eye as she leaned back and made herself comfortable in the rocker. Lifting me up onto her lap, she softly brushed a strand of hair from my face. Rocking gently for a moment she got a 'Far Away' look on her face, then said; "Once upon a time, eons ago, in the kingdom of the misty 'Thule the Hidden' realm, the first Monarch ever, had a gorgeous newborn. Her rainbow-hued hair was in tight curly ringlets and sat on her head like a coronet. She had four-color freckles all over her opaque body; an extremely unique looking baby." Sigga stopped, then continued.

"The King and Queen decided that they must choose an exceptional name for their child but they had been warned by the elf Queen, Borghildur of Álaborg, that a certain tröll was planning to do a 'changeling' attack, that is, sneak into the palace and switch the King's baby with a tröll baby and this way take over their land. She suggested a secret name and the King heeded her advice and named their baby a secret name. No one knew that name except the baby's Guardian Angel. The name would be kept secret until the end of days. But the name that she was known by was Snotra. This was an elf name that would be a charm and protect the child all through her life."

She stopped again for a moment, took a deep breath and with a piercing look at me said; "Perhaps your mother heard of this and gave you an unusual name, for a charm and good luck."

"Sigga!" Auntie started. The chair legs tottered and clattered as she abruptly stood up. She stopped when Sigga glared at her.

"And the kids at school? What do they know? Pouf, to their opinion and name calling, and give it to the trölls!" She waved her hand and snapped her fingers.

Wow, I loved this woman! Hah, when I get back to school, and they start the teasing, I'll just say, "I give your opinions to the trölls!" I bet that'll scare them witless!

Simply delicious, I could hardly wait! In just a few moments, this woman I'd just met took care of my name-dilemma just like that! [I tried to snap my fingers... I'll have to learn to do that!]

I scooted off Sigga's lap and ran for the door. I had to share this with Finna! Then I turned and gave Sigga a fierce hug until she grunted, then laughed.

"Diddamín, remember not to take this story seriously." Aunt Þórbjörg called after me, looking very concerned.

"Oh, but it's very good, and the kids don't know if it's true or not, we have so many stories like this, but this one is simply the best!" I giggled as I sped out the door.

My grin stayed plastered on my face as I clambered all the way up the cliff. Wadding my skirt around my knees, I raced to Finna's house.

I liked Finna. She had lots of shiny, auburn, hair. Her blue-green eyes sparkled with merriment. We were the same age, but she was three inches taller and somewhat heavier than I was. Her mother had died when she was very small, she didn't remember her at all. Her father was a good shoemaker but a stern, taciturn and opinionated man. He had not married again. About Ólafur's age, he had none of his tact, or gentleness, especially when it came to talking politics. Kristján was of the opinion that the "government should see to it that everyone has the same in life."

I remember a community meeting where Kristján started his usual "the government isn't taking care of people like they should" rant. Things got heated as men took sides. Ólafur tried to soothe the tempers. But Kristján got purple-faced and belligerent. Finally, Grandpa, just as belligerent as Kristján, stood up and shouted that one should work hard and *earn* their way, not just be handed *stuff* on a "silver platter." This was like waving a red flag in the face of an angry bull, and brought on a free-for-all, as they got into fierce arguments over this.

Then Grandpa threw up his hand and told Kristán "I suppose if some people are born more beautiful than others, you'll want to cut off their noses to 'even up everyone's looks'!" Then he stomped out of the meeting.

Finna listened to me with as much glee as I had with Sigga. Dancing around the room, she chanted, "I kept telling you your mother gave you a name that is unique!"

Then she stopped, a pensive look came on her face as she murmured, "I miss not having a mother. I want to go to the country-dance that's coming up, but I have outgrown my dresses. I have fabric but I can't cut it out on myself. Dad can't do it." She paused, then cocked her head at me and asked, "Will you cut it for me?"

I had made quite a few doll clothes for sock-dolls, and at ten years of age was rather adept with the sewing-needle. I wasn't sure I could do this, but looking into the wistful face of my friend I knew I had to try.

I contoured the fabric on her body and pinned it in place, then cut all around her. Scraps fell to the floor as I re-fitted and re-pinned and snipped away. After the cutting, we sewed the whole dress by hand, we didn't have a sewing-machine.

The dress turned out quite pretty, and we attended the dance where we had a great time taking turns dancing with old men, young men, women and girls. The old wood floor buckled and popped under our energetic, polka-stomping, feet.

Sitting down for a spell to catch my breath, my head swiveled side to side as I watched the twirling dancers, and Björssi's flying fingers on the accordion. My cousin Nonni, from Hámundarstaðir, was trying to keep up on drums Björssi had fashioned out of sealskin, tightened over a wood barrel. Keeping fair time with a couple of sticks, he was making plenty of thumping noises until he decided to join the ring of dancers.

Clapping my hands in rhythm with the music, I thought back to last year when Lilla, Sísí and I were here on this dance floor. A man, about Ólafur's age, had come over and asked Lilla for a dance. She was too shy. Ducking her head, she'd turned away. Later the man came back and, with a big grin, handed her a twine-twisted ring and told her it was a called a 'bashful ring.'

Shyly, she put it on then twisted her hand this way and that, proudly admiring the ring when Sísí told her she should dance at least one dance with the man. She looked up at the guy, still standing by, and slowly nodded her head. The next thing we knew she was clear across the floor hopping like crazy in a riotous polka, his five kids circling and dancing around them. We knew the man's eleven year-old son, Grímur had been wanting to meet Lilla, but he too, was also very shy. We joked about this for the longest time, but we also thought it was a clever way of giving Grímur a chance to dance with my little sister.

I got up, smoothed down my skirt and grabbed Nonni's hand as he came flying by me. We all went twirling faster and faster until everyone was out of breath. Mercifully the music stopped.

"Coffee-time!" Laughing and hooting we gathered around the table piled high with cheese, dried cod, smoked mutton, and more. Vienna tort, pancakes, twist-cookies, and, of course, coffee and fire-wine [for the adult males.]

Finna came up behind me, smiling, cheeks beet-red, grabbing my waist she whispered,

"Thanks for helping with my dress, Teitur sure likes it." He was a boy that Finna had liked forever.

We danced almost through the whole night. None of us wanted to waste the day-bright nights of the short summer.

Íeda Jónasdóttir Herman

What a wonderful time we had. We were ten and life was good.

Vopnafjörður 1915
From left to right: Uncle Helgi, Amma Sigríður, Aunt Þorbjörg, Afi Björn and Pabbi Jónas

Chapter 14

Hámundarstaðir
Grandpa's Farm

Squinting and shading my eyes, I searched the white-capped ocean waves for Grandpa's small, black and white fishing boat. Cocking my head, I tried to hear the *chug-chug* of the motor over the screeching of seagulls and the slapping of the ocean swells against the rocks. I watched as patches of gray fog twirled over the choppy waves in the formidable northern Fjord. Leaning forward, I scrunched my eyes almost shut, but I saw no sign of his boat. After the dance the night before, I'd slept late and Grandpa had gone back to Vopnafjörður.

Standing on the edge of the distorted, odd-shaped lava cliff, I felt the grounds tremble and heard the powerful ocean crashing and rumbling up the gorge. Swooshing, sucking sounds came from deep within the cave the ocean waves had carved eons past.

Scrambling down a gravelly crevasse, I dug in my heels and my fingers gripped the gritty, sharp lava ledges. Scattered clumps of heather bravely tried to find roots in small beds of smooth, volcanic ash, the small pink and white flowers contrasting oddly with the blue-grey surrealistic surrounding.

The racket of rolling stones alarmed the nesting puffins, warily they pointed toward me with their huge red, yellow, and black striped beaks. Shaking their short wings and portly bodies, they waddled off on their fiery-red feet.

I touched a moss-lined seagull's nest, which promptly came alive with necks stretching and twitching, hungry mouths wide open. I jerked my hand back as the angry mama bird streaked down like a meteorite, yellow beak wide open, screaming fiercely.

Carefully avoiding white streaks of yucky bird droppings and inching my way to the bottom of the cliff I started running on the narrow strip of gray-black volcanic sand. My sheepskin shoes made squishy, slushy sounds as small waves wet my feet. Gross smells arose when I kicked against slimy patches of algae and hopped around carcasses of birds, crabs, brittle fish bones and blue seashells.

Stopping for a moment, I leaned against a half-buried relic of a rowboat. Pulling at the coarse brown fishnet that hung over the rotted bulwark, I disturbed five napping Harbors seals. They looked at me with their brown, marble-shiny eyes, then moaning, groaning and grumbling they closed their eyes.

Tugging the seaman's yellow rain-hat tight over my hair I tried to avoid bird droppings, as a gazillion seagulls swept overhead.

The wispy shreds of fog across the water were slowly dissipating as the sun broke through the clouds. A brilliant gold, red and blue colored rainbow curved over a tall misty waterfall. Rivers and brooks cascaded down the jagged, immense, snow-capped mountain sheltering the fjord.

I climbed to my favorite place, the top of a barnacle-crusted lava rock accessible on one side in the outgoing tide. Waves caused spray to slosh on my face and sting my cheeks. Licking my lips, I tasted the salt water.

A fog-shrouded steamship made its way across the mouth of the fjord. The warning blast of the ship's foghorn boomed mournfully between the basalt-black towering cliffs.

Powerful spouts from Humpback whales dotted the sea. They slapped their long flippers, roiled the water and made it difficult to spot Grandpa's small boat.

Gray seals shot up out of the ocean, grabbing squirming fish from the beaks of diving gulls. The seals' bodies glistened and shone like well-polished whale bone as they leaped up and then dove back into the waves. For a while I watched, mesmerized, then searched the fjord again, my stomach churned. I knew well the deadly perils of the sea. I'd heard that Íngi and his crew had drowned in Seyðisfjörður, shortly after our ship had turned north. I shuddered at the thought of how close we were to seeing that happen.

Dragging my feet, I turned back. A virtual blizzard of seagulls and puffins floated below the fluffy clouds in the gray-blue sky above my head. Slowly I climbed back up the bird-filled lava cliff.

"Come on everybody. Down to the dock!" I heard Uncle Bjössi shout.

Reaching the top, I spotted the boat a little way out. White froth sprayed out like wings at the bow as the boat swooped up and down in the choppy water. Leaping to my feet, I ran to catch up with my uncle, grandma, and her summer help, Þóra. All of us whooping and running as we headed down to the dilapidated dock.

The pilings were old, barnacle-covered, and rotting in places, but still strong enough to hold us as we ran. The wet uneven planks bounced up and down by our clomping feet and made small bait-bucket rattle. A tattered old fishnet shook as Bjössi ran then tossed to Grandpa the end of a coiled up rope fastened to an old rusty motor.

Catching the rope with his right hand, Grandpa's gnarled left hand held tight on the wheel as he brought the rocking fishing boat to the dock with experienced ease. We started to unload the large, heavy bags of flour, sugar and other supplies, and as always, fighting off the screeching, greedy, diving seagulls.

Grandpa was safe.

Chapter 15

Cows Go Crazy in the Spring

It was a sunny day for a change. A rare, warm, breeze was blowing in from the ocean, causing the salty air to bring faint smell of musty algae and spring weeds.

Björn was ready to let the cows out for the first time this Spring. Old Rauða, Hilda, and the heifer, Freyja, were restlessly two stepping in their stalls.

I stood outside with my cousins from the farm, Hámundarstaðir II. Nonni (his name was Jónas, but there were so many Jónases already in the family that he was nicknamed Nonni), who was twelve. He had sky-blue eyes, sparkling with mischief, adventurous and outgoing; his sister Dóra, cautious and timid, while the younger sister, Sigga, was a bit of both: cautious and spontaneous.

Grandpa called them *The Three Golden Gremlins*, because all looked alike with almost identical hair color – golden yellow - and where you saw one, you saw the other two.

"Alright, come in and get ready," Bjossi hollered from inside the cow-house.

I got ready to tiptoe around the cow's manure, but Björn had cleaned the dung-trench.

"I... I don't want to do this, I... I just want to watch." Dóra stuttered, cringing.

"Ok, Nonni, you can have Hilda. Sigga you take Freyja, and Diddamín, you take old Rauða, you know her and her mean ways!" Bjössi chuckled.

Just outside the front door, Grand-amma was sitting on a three-legged stool. Grandma Sigríður was perched on the hitching rock. Þóra stood by, arms akimbo, eyebrows knit in a heavy frown.

The show was about to begin. The one who held their cow's tail the longest was the winner!

Nonni, Sigga and I had stationed ourselves behind our respective cow, firmly grabbing a tail. The cows mooed and twisted their heads to look at us, at the same time trying to swish their tails.

Old Rauða was getting riled, her hind feet started stomping from side to side.

"Hurry, open the door!" I jumped away from a hoof aimed at my legs.

"I have to untie them. Dad will open the door when I yell," Bjössi was scrambling at the hay-trough lifting the ropes off the cows' heads.

"Ok, Dad!" Bjössi hollered. The door opened with a screechy-creaking noise, not having been opened all winter.

Suddenly it was as if a fox had jumped into the cow-house. The cows backed out every which way trying to get outside and at the same time feeling the pull we kids had on their tails.

Freyja started out first. The heifer stopped and stared, wild-eyed. Sigga was tugging the tail, screaming and urging the heifer to move. Nonni was next with Hilda dragging him on a fast run; his long, skinny legs were wildly pumping up and down. His hollering and yelling startled the heifer, which scrambled outside and yanked Sigga off her feet. She let go of the tail and Freyja took off jumping and bucking.

Old Rauða rolled her eyes at me then viciously kicked back. Turning as if she was a teen-cow, she took off out of the cow-house at a clumsy, kick-hopping clop.

I could hear the adults laughing and egging us on. Björssi was whooping like a cowboy herding cattle. I glanced sideways and saw that Sigga had let go and the heifer was clomping into the field. I could hear Nonni almost catching up. Then I tripped and fell on my stomach, I bit into gritty dust but still held on while Rauða dragged me on the ground. She was kicking and bucking like an ill-mannered horse. My mouth was getting full of dirt and grass, mixed with blood from my slit lip, but I was not about to let go!

"Stop, you've won! LET GO! LET GO!" Everyone was screaming at the same time. Gritting my teeth, my fingers were frozen in a stubborn death grip as sharp, lava pebbles stung my cheeks. Rauða did a turn-around, and I swung in a big arch, let go of the tail and tumbled into the creek where we did our laundry, and washed the wool after the sheep were shorn.

I sat in the ice-cold water, steaming-hot temper at a full boil. I was a bloody, dirty mess and old Rauða had gotten the best of me. She stopped and looked at me. I swear she smirked as she rolled her big, brown, cow-eyes at me again. Mumbling a soft 'Moo' she nonchalantly ambled after the other cows, stopping now and then to curl her long tongue around little tufts of fresh grass.

I was infuriated. I didn't mind a horse dumping me, but a cow... !?!

The whole family came running, hysterically laughing, although my two grandmas were concerned. Björssi jumped into the creek with a rag in his hand and proceeded to mop off the blood on my face as he pulled me up to my feet.

"She's fine, just madder than a wet hen." Björssi chortled, as I spit out a sliver of lava-shale.

"You'd be mad too if a *cow* dumped *you* into the creek!" I spit out the words and glared at my uncle, who kept dabbing at my face, grinning.

"You should have let go!" Nonni wiped tears from his eyes with the back of his left hand, while still doubled up with laughter.

"Yeah, why didn't you just let go?" Sigga and Dóra giggled.

I started shivering, and then mumbled, "Just get me outta here!"

"Here Björssi, wrap her up in my shawl." Grandma Sigríður handed him her black lopi-wrap. As we walked up to the farm, my sheepskin shoes made slushy, squeaky sound in harmony with the *slop-slop* of Björssi's water-filled, seal-skin boots. I turned and looked grimly at Rauða. She was totally oblivious of me, contently chewing her cud.

With much merriment, we all got to the farm where Þóra suddenly jumped out of the door. Looking at my scratched-up face, she exclaimed "Good heavens girl, don't you EVER learn?!" She softened her words by giving me a soft thump on the shoulder. Quickly she dabbed her eyes with the corner of her shawl. "Come on, Diddamín, let's get some hot drink into your tummy." I was touched by her obvious concern and patted her hand.

After a cup of hot coffee and a batch of twist-cookies, I got my humor back. I laughed along with the others as each one took a turn in describing the event, each one trying to outdo the other, laughing and slapping their knees.

"I think you all are just plum crazy." Muttered Dora. "I thought you all were going to get killed! That old cow, Rauða, with her sharp, pointy horns and mean eyes, is the most wicked-looking thing!"

"Well, the old 'thing' doesn't have the best temper in the ruminant world, but her horns sure are beauties." Grandpa had a dreamy look on his face. I wondered if he was thinking of a new snuff-horn! I realized that her horns *did* have striking markings: black-brown streaks on ivory bone. Those horns would make a very handsome tobacco-holder; very likely could be the envy of the local farmers who competed for the most colorful and ornate "snuffy".

"Tomorrow we'll start shearing the sheep before turning them out." Grandpa rubbed his chin, twirled his mustache and squinted at my three cousins. "You Gremlins want to come over for some fun and work? We'll have eighteen ewes and four rams to shear and a few lambs to earmark."

"Don't forget we'll also be washing the wool in the creek." Grandma motioned to the kids with her cup of coffee.

"We'd love to help!" Nonni, enthusiastically, spoke for his two sisters as they nodded. "We'll be back in the morning then!" They headed out the door, waving and hollering.

"Bless, bless!"

Chapter 16

Shearing Time

We were gathered by the fast-running, gurgling creek where I'd been dumped the day before. The sun was shining, although not very bright or warm, it *was* lurking in the thin, raggedy clouds. I hoped, for the sheep's sake, that it would warm up. They were sure to feel cold when shorn of their wooly coats.

The fire was roaring, devouring the dry peat-and-cow chips. Steam from the iron kettle curled up into the cool air, and grey-white mist swirled over the bubbles rolling in the water. Þóra dropped in a handful of green, homemade, lye soap. The effect was like the gushing of Little Geyser, shooting up into the air.

Þóra and Grandma were sitting on lava rocks that were softly cushioned by thick, silver-grey moss. Grand-Amma and Dóra were sitting on wood stools just outside the sheepcote, carefully situated out of the way when the door would swing open and Bjössi, Grandpa, and Nonni would come out with a sheep, hands firmly holding the horns. Sigga and I stood by with the shears in our hands, like nurses in an operating room; *knife-scalpel-scissors*. The men came out, each one straddling a sheep. When Grandpa stumbled and let go of the ewe, Sigga managed to grab a handful of stringy, dirty wool, slowing the sheep down enough for me to grab the horns and frantically hold on. Swinging my leg over her squirming back, I squeezed her between my knees and dug my heels into the ground. Sigga let go as Grandpa grabbed the shears from her hand and took over the horns, twisting the sheep's head to one side and forcing her to lie down. I sat down by her head and held her tight, she kicked her feet a bit and let out a plaintive "bah." Grandpa was quick and the sheep was speedily shorn. As I let her up, she vigorously shook her head and body. I wondered if she felt as ridiculous as she looked!

Grandpa went in for the next one. Nonni was done shearing, and Sigga let go of the sheep she was holding for him.

"Yow! Get the ram!" I heard Björssi yell in a weird voice.

The ludicrous, half-shorn ram was wriggling, and clumsily waddling down the field, his feet tangling up in the wool dragging on the ground. Björssi was crouched on the ground grabbing his crotch trying to get his breath back. The rest of us ran and formed a circle, slowly forcing the ram to get closer to the sheepcote. Björssi was staggering to his feet, slaughter in his eyes. He was okay. I didn't dare ask: *Who is madder than a wet hen now?*

The shearing was done swiftly. Now it was time to mark the lambs. I felt sorry for them as Grandpa cut his two V-marks in the left ear. I noticed Sigga and Dóra averted their eyes as the bright-red blood dribbled down, and stained the lambs' curly wool. I knew farmers had to mark their sheep, but wished there was an easier way of doing that.

When the hot water was ready, we gathered some of the sheared, dirty wool and pitched it into the boiling water. Using long-handled wood poles, Grandpa and Björssi stirred and then lifted the heavy, wet fleece out of the black kettle and into the, sparkling, clear creek. My cousins and I jumped into the ice-cold water and rinsed out any residue of soap. Then the women spread the wool on the ground to dry.

Later we gathered the wool and brought it inside. We kept it in a corner of the kitchen, where Grandma had her spinning wheel. A skein of spun brown yarn was looped over the spindle. Above the spinning wheel was a wood shelf with a clutter of

Íeda Jónasdóttir Herman

books, and a collection of snuff-horns displayed among the volumes. An oil lamp sat in the middle of the table with its chimney clean and shiny from Þóra's obsessive washing.

Grand-Amma took the skein off the spinning wheel and draped the loop across my hands; I spread them apart so the skein wouldn't droop as she started to wind the yarn into a ball. As days went by, Grandma Sigríður, Þóra and I would comb the new wool, while grand-Amma would spin it into desired yarn thickness.

Icelandic sheep wool has an inner, fine undercoat and a coarser outer-coat. We knitted the soft Lopi sweaters from the soft inner fleece that grand-Amma just barely spun, this was called "*lopi*." The outer wool she spun into tight, strong yarn from which we knitted mittens, socks and *leppar*, which were inner-soles for our sheepskin shoes, and usually a child's first knitting project.

Spinning wheels, wool-cards (combs) and looms were a necessary part of Grandma's household equipment.

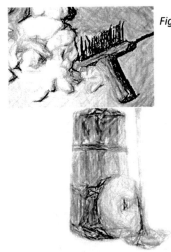

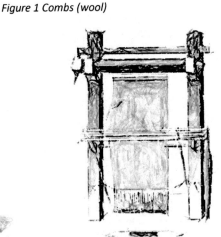

Figure 1 Combs (wool)

Figure 2 Butter Churn

Figure 3 Vertical Loom

Chapter 17

Grandpa Hires Summer Help

The hustle and the bustle on the day Grandpa got ready to hire summer help was nothing short of amazing. I was shooed from one corner to another while Grandma and Þóra swept, scrubbed and cleaned.

Strong aroma of green coffee beans browning in a black kettle that hung over the fireplace permeated the kitchen. I loved the smell of coffee, and one of my favorite chores was to grind the coffee in the wooden coffee mill. Every so often, I'd pull out the boxy drawer at the bottom of the mill and sniff deeply, blissfully, as the ground coffee accumulated.

I watched as Grandma filled the blue and white speckled, chipped, coffeepot with boiling water. When she dropped in a handful of coffee and a pinch of chicory, the water in the pot erupted hissing and steaming like a miniature volcano.

A large, black, kettle was on the back burner of the kitchen stove. Delicious whiffs of the mutton soup that was simmering in it made my mouth water. All day, bits of mutton-meat, potato, carrots and rutabaga were added. Coffee and soup simmering away, all day, was a tradition with Grandma.

"Diddamín, we are almost out of sand to scrub the floor." Grandma handed me a grey, beat-up, metal bucket. "Run down and get some. And get Snati and Goldie to chase the sheep off the roof."

I looked at the floor that, to me, was clean enough to eat off.

The boards were white as could be from numerous, down-on-our-knees, scrubbing with rough scoria. But if Grandma said it needed scrubbing, it needed scrubbing!

Running across the rock-scattered field, I scrambled down the lava cliff, deliberately making scraping racket with the bucket just to startle the starchy, important acting puffins. They seemed so unflappable. I wondered how it would feel to be a puffin, or seagull, or a kría, just floating ever so smoothly up in the air, without a care. And here I came messing up their lives. I felt a small twinge of remorse; I didn't like to have *my* life messed up every Spring and every Fall.

I'd been shipped from Reykjavik to Vopnafjörður and back again as long as I could remember. I loved the fjord, and didn't like to have to go back to the city. *I can go to school here just as well*, I thought, slamming the bucket on the rocks, driving hundreds of seagulls into the air, screaming fiercely. They dove at me in a fit of temper before settling back on the lichen- and moss-covered lava ledges.

Filling the bucket with the volcanic sand, I stood for a moment watching the hypnotic slow-moving, blue-green, waves slapping the shiny-wet black rocks. Long strings of yellow-brownish algae floated slowly. Up and down, up and down, up and down.

The fjord was calm today.

"Halló child. What's keeping you?" Þóra leaned precariously over the edge, her shrill voice echoed and bounced off the cliffs causing the seagulls again to fly off into the air, screeching manically.

"I'm coming, I'm coming," I hollered back.

"I declare, you're the most day-dreaming child I've ever met!" She yelled in an aggravated voice.

After I scrambled back up the cliff, Þóra grabbed the bucket from my hand and ran toward the house. "Don't forget the sheep; your Grandma wants them off the roof before company arrives."

I got Snati and Goldie to chase the protesting sheep off the turf-roof and then ran inside. Quietly slipping past the busy women, I sped up the rickety stairs to my favorite place in the whole wide world, *Grandpa's attic*. This area had an aroma all of its own, musty papers, old leather, and tobacco. Even the salty, tangy smell of the ocean found its way into the attic room.

Grandpa had literally hundreds of books lined floor to ceiling, wall to wall, heaped on a table, on top of his massive desk, and even stacked on the windowsill. I couldn't walk a straight line in the room, but had to meander around books and old, yellowing, newspapers with curled edges and piled up on the floor in a haphazard manner.

Those papers were something else! I once asked Grandpa why he had saved all these old papers, many written in English. I knew he was uncomfortable speaking the language, but read it with ease.

"I read about families, like your Grandma's sister, Guðríður, who emigrated to Manitoba, Canada. She, her family, and many others left after the world's worse volcano eruption happened here in Iceland. The Laki eruption in 1784 ruined much of the countryside and for years made living extremely difficult." As Grandpa picked up a paper, fine dust flittered to the floor.

"This here is called The Heimskringlan, printed in Winnipeg. It's written in Icelandic and tells where some of the Icelanders settled, many on an island called Gimli, Manitoba. All of these books and papers are like good friends. I read and enjoy them again and again, I wouldn't part with any of them." He fondly patted the stack of papers.

I don't remember any "children's" books but all the stories of the Vikings came to life in that attic. This was pure heaven for the bookworm that I was. I loved reading the *SAGAS* and *EDDA*, written by one of our ancestors, Snorri Sturluson (1178-1241). Our country was so isolated from the rest of the world that our language had not changed much. I was able to read the old writings with ease.

Grandpa and I were alike in reading more Icelandic history than anything else. We had some lively discussions about the Vikings, their travels, discoveries, and so-called murderous bloodthirsty ways. Many Vikings were farmers. They also were skilled navigators and sailors. Of course I was *ALWAYS* taught that Leifur Eirikursson [another well-known ancestor, this one on mother's side according to her] discovered America 500 years before Columbus!

"Child come down here!" Þóra´s thunderous voice shattered my solitude. I should have known that she'd seen me slip upstairs. I was sure she had eyes in the back of her head!

"I have to brush your hair before company arrives!" She thumped the wood ceiling for emphasis.

I'm ten, as if I couldn't brush and braid my own hair! Fuming I scrambled to my feet. The books on the floor bounced as she thumped again, harder this time. I didn't mess around but flew down stairs and jumped on the three-legged wooden stool she'd set out for me. Undoing my long black braids, my hazel eyes watered as she firmly brushed out the tangles. Grimacing and pursing her lips, she gave me her no-nonsense look as her ample bosom bobbed up and down with each stroke.

Grandma Sigríður, who was short and slim, sat on a stool that Grandpa had built just for her. She sat with the butter churn firmly held in place by her skinny knees. Her black skirt and long white apron hiked up revealed black, woolen stockings. She had both hands clamped on the wooden butter-pole, hand over hand. The churn slurped and sloshed as Grandma, energetically, pumped up and down, making the sleeves on her blouse flop and flounce.

Great-Grandma sat in the corner rocking back and forth and knitting so fast I couldn't see the points of the four, clicking, needles. The metal needles made fascinating click-clack rhythm sounds as the sock she was knitting took shape.

"Why are you knitting so fast Grand-Amma?" My eyes followed the fast-moving needles with fascination.

Finishing a row, she pulled out one needle, and pushed an escaped tuft of white hair back under the black cap she always wore. The cap had a long tassel, reaching from her left ear down past her shoulder, a carved three-inch silver cylinder placed close to the cap kept the strands from separating. Like Grandma and Þóra, she wore a long skirt and an apron tied at the waist.

She had on a black vest intricately embroidered with silver thread, and laced up at the front with a silver chain that hung over her bosom. The vest was similar to the other women's Sunday clothes but great-Grandma wore "dress-ups" every day, except during haying time when the men worked close to the farm, at which time she would not wear the ornate vest, but a brown and white knitted *lopi* sweater. She'd kind of waddle out to help rake and turn the rows of hay.

Scratching her head with the needle, she quizzically looked at me. She had a habit of cocking her head to one side and closing her left blue eye, while opening wide her right, brown eye.

"I want to get this sock done before I run out of yarn." Grinning she held up a slowly disappearing ball of yarn, and then looked up into the faces of chuckling Grandma and Þóra.

"But Grand-Amma... " She was teasing me, it was the same amount of yarn used whether she knitted fast or slow. Þóra was finished and I got off the stool in a huff and went to look for Grandpa. I could hear him in the guest room, blowing his nose. A rake was lying on the floor, across the doorway. I picked it up and leaned it against the wall.

"You're hired!" Grandpa's voice boomed.

I jumped "What? Oh, Grandpa, I bet you could be heard all the way outside!"

"Diddamín, I've taught you right!" Grandpa gleefully slapped and rubbed wrinkled, red hands on his knees. "I'm getting ready to hire summer workers and I laid the rake there as a test. If a person steps over it, I will not hire them. The same goes if they kick it aside, but if they do what you just did, it's an indication of a good worker. I learned that from my Father who learned it from his father. It has worked well for us for generations!" He chuckled and blew his nose again.

"Grandpa, you're funny." I loved both my grandparents, but I 'took after' Grandpa more than Grandma, just as I 'took after' my somber, brown-eyed, black haired Father more than my Mother did.

Grandpa had very thick black hair now peppered with gray. Bushy eyebrows over keen dark brown eyes and a handlebar, graying mustache that he had a habit of twirling when meditating, or working on endless math problems. Besides reading, he had a passion for math. Papers, scribbled with fraction problems, were scattered about wherever he rested for a bit. I thought that was strange, I didn't like math at all!

"I heard the butter-churn sloshing, and now I smell newly baked bread." Grandpa scrunched his nose, sniffed, tilted his head back and roared.

"How about some coffee and fresh bread, Þóra!"

Grandma's blue figurine-painted china was already on the table that was handsomely covered with a white tablecloth that she had embroidered in an intricate "cut-out" design. Grandma *always* put out her best for company; after all, they were few and far between in this rugged, remote fjord, situated in the north-east coast of Iceland, not far from the arctic circle.

Þóra brought in the coffee, scrumptious hot bread and a bowl of butter. Grandpa poured part of his coffee into the cup's saucer, then he held the small dish between his hands and blew on the drink to cool, then he took a sip. I watched him for moment, and then imitated him. Grandpa chuckled as he reached over and tore off two thick pieces of the hot bread and smeared on big slabs of butter that melted, and ran down the sides and onto the dish.

We sat by the window and looked at the mountain bathed in rare rays of golden-red light, and made the blue-green ocean glimmer and shimmer. I saw our reflections in the glass. So did Grandpa. His eyes crinkled at the corners as he smiled at me and nodding his head, reading my mind.

"Diddamín, there is no place like this." He said, softly.

Contently sipping my coffee from the china cup and looking at our reflections in the window glass, I whole-heartedly agreed. I wanted to stay here, like this, forever!

We heard the yipping of the dogs, neighing of horses, and cheery greetings.

Company had arrived.

Chapter 18

Hanna

I ran outside in time to see Helgi, whom I'd met last year, dismount and grab Bjössi in a bear hug.

"Good to see you, Helgi." Bjössi suddenly stopped. Staring at Helgi's companion the, normally, glib Uncle of mine seemed at a loss for words. Then, somewhat haltingly, he asked,

"Is this your cousin you said wanted to work for Dad this summer?" Bjössi eyes were glued on the young lady that swung her slim legs gracefully off of her horse, a lazy looking, cross-eyed roan. The young woman looked about eighteen to twenty, and was very attractive. She wore loose fitting long trousers that looked more like a split skirt. Her white sweater was knit in the usual intricate Icelandic pattern. In her hand, she held a whip with an elaborately designed silver handle.

Her beautiful blond hair was in braids that wound around on top of her head like a golden crown that almost gave her an ethereal demeanor. She had wide open, violet-blue, eyes that didn't miss much, like the admiring looks from Uncle Bjössi, who was about the same age. She gave me a slow, right-eye wink, which reminded me of Sólveig. I loved her right away and tried to figure how I could give her a hint about grandpa's test. I couldn't think of anything; I just fervently hoped she would pick up the rake before she entered the room.

"Welcome Jóhanna Jóhannessdóttir, come on in," Grandpa called.

"Blessings on your home. Glad to meet you, Björn Jónasson.

Please call me Hanna, my mother is Jóhanna." She smiled as she started to step inside. Stopping, she reached down and picked up the rake and leaned it carefully against the wall. Grinning from ear to ear I peeked around her and caught Grandpa's face. I *knew* we had new help.

Turning around, I almost tripped over Bjössi's feet. He and Helgi had followed close behind me and Bjössi couldn't take his eyes off the new girl. I saw Helgi look at Bjössi. An oddly sad, small, smile curved his lips. I thought about that for a moment then shook my head; I'm letting my silly imagination run wild again! Grandpa stood up and shook Hanna's hand motioning for her and Helgi to sit down.

"Diddamín, ask Þóra to bring us some more bread and coffee." Grandpa said with a humorous glint in his eyes as he observed Bjössi's reaction to the girl. I thought Grandpa himself was acting a little strange. He usually tilted his head back in his chair and bellowed for his coffee. Now he was being quite the gentleman! I went to speak with Þóra.

As the adults visited, I watched Helgi´s cousin with curiosity, especially because of Bjössi´s obvious interest. Uncle Bjössi was an accomplished accordion player, and was much sought after to play at weddings and country-dance in nearby villages, and outdoor gatherings like the Fall sheep-roundup. With his quick mischievous smile, bright blue eyes, auburn hair and broad shoulders, he was very popular with the young ladies, but hadn't been particularly interested in any one of them. I had always thought of him as an adult, but now he became just as goofy as the boys at school who liked to yank on my braids. Hanna didn't seem interested in Bjössi. Her soft, serene glance was the same for all of us.

Grandpa told Hanna that she was hired, and after a short visit, Helgi took off for their family farm. Þóra showed Hanna where she would be staying while working on the farm.

I was old enough to help the adults with the haying but had a hard time keeping up with Hanna who was a whirlwind of a worker, like Guðrún was last year. Furiously raking the rows of hay, Hanna caused the dry grass to whirl up in the air as in a strong, northern, gale. I thought she worked too hard. Every so often, she'd lean over and take a strange gulping breath. I wanted to say something to Grandpa, but she gave me a warning look as she shook her head and put a finger to her lip then went back to raking with intense determination. I don't know if Helgi knew of Grandpa´s test and told Hanna.

But Grandpa's test was good anyway.

Chapter 19

Do Horses and Dogs Have 'ESP' ?

"Aren't we ready to go? They are here, we'll miss the tide if we don't hurry!" I shouted to Hanna who was still inside the house. I was outside, watching my three girl friends from the nearby farmsteads arrive. Gréta, who was ten, Unnur, eleven, and her ten-year old sister, Sína, were grinning from ear to ear in anticipation as the horses came, pell-mell, across the field.

"Hi, shall we dismount?" Unnur asked, as her horse came to a rearing stop.

"Hi. I don't think you need to." I greeted the girls. "I just hollered for Hanna, she should be right out." I finished adjusted the stirrups on my saddle, then turned to the house, a little puzzled, wondering what Hanna was doing.

Their horses snorted, impatiently chewed at the bits and pranced around. My horse, Stjarna, the oldest and laziest of them all, danced about, eager to take off. But Bjössi's horse, Thunder, was almost subdued. I'd never seen him like this. Thunder was well known for his competitive nature, and couldn't stand to have another horse in front of him. He was the fastest runner in our county, and Bjössi proudly displayed several of their racing awards in his room.

We were going swimming in a geothermal-warm swim hole on the other side of the fjord's inlet and Hanna was planning to ride Thunder for the trip. Her cross-eyed horse was getting old and stayed pretty much out in the pasture until needed at haying time.

I sure hoped Bjössi's horse wasn't sick, not just for his sake, but the other horses were way out in the outer field, and I was afraid we'd miss the outgoing tide if we had to go and get another horse, which would mean riding the long way around instead of crossing the inlet. And that could mean losing what little sun we might have for our swim.

Darting inside I called for Bjössi. He and grandpa were at the kitchen table drinking coffee.

"Would you both come out and look at Thunder? He isn't acting like himself!" I said, as a flutter of unease churned in my stomach.

Bjössi shot up out of his seat. The chair teetered for a moment before tumbling over and skittering on the wood floor. Both he and Grandpa dashed outside. Carefully they ran their hands over the horse, looked into his eyes, and checked his mouth. Grandpa carefully examined Hanna's saddle. Thunder tossed his head at the close inspection. Now swishing his tail, he nuzzled Bjössi then started his usual prancing around eager for a run; he sure seemed to have recovered mighty quickly!

Hanna stepped out of the door and walked up to Thunder, who nervously shied away from her. Her hair was in two long braids and hung almost down to her waist; she looked so pretty. Swinging her right braid over her shoulder, she cocked her head, puzzled.

"This is the first time Thunder has acted like he didn't like my saddle, or even me!" she murmured, sadly.

"I'll just take him for a quick run and see how he does" Bjössi jumped into Hanna's saddle. The stirrups were too short, but he managed to scrunch up his legs and off they went at a brisk gallop across the grassy field. Then Thunder went into his famous tölt and from there into flying pace; a pace unique to Icelandic horses, where the horse moves both legs of one side at the same time. Bjössi and his horse became as one in a spectacular flying form. Thunder's bronze coat with the black mane, glistened in the sun, black tail plumed out behind him and his four black socks were a blur.

"Not a thing wrong with that horse." Grandpa proclaimed proudly. Thunder was born on Grandpa's farm when Bjössi was twelve. His dad had given him the colt with the understanding that my uncle would have complete charge in taking care of him and train him. Bjössi had done an outstanding job and Grandpa was justifiably proud of both his son and horse.

"Thunder is fine, Hanna, just a little temperamental when I'm not the one in the saddle. I guess I have him a little spoiled. It'll do him good to get used to you."

All the way to the inlet, Thunder stayed behind the other horses. This was so unusual I couldn't help but keep looking back. Thunder behind Stjarna? Unbelievable. Strange foreboding crept down my spine. The three girls had already entered the inlet, giggling as the cold water sprayed over their legs. Stjarna was just going in when I heard Hanna's voice.

"Jump up here, old boy." She patted the back of her saddle as Grandpa and Bjössi had often done before. But Snati whimpered and stuck his tail between his legs. To my astonishment, the old dog took a flying leap and landed on Stjarna, right behind me!

I looked at Hanna, and her face was ashen. She looked like she'd seen a ghost.

"What's the matter, Hanna?" I whispered, looking around, scared. The three girls' horses were plodding ahead, sloshing a great deal of water as they went across the bay.

"It's nothing, I just felt funny for a minute. I think Thunder and Snati have me spooked!" Her laugh seemed a little forced.

"Maybe we should wait to go swimming, Hanna." I thought she looked really ill.

All of a sudden, Thunder decided it was time to move. Wading in, he took off more like his old self and almost galloped in the water! Stjarna followed at a more sedate pace. I could hear the girls' laughter and the pounding hoofs of the horses as they got out of the water and onto the ground, then took off at a brisk canter. Our horses sloshed across the inlet, and we reached the other side, where both horses acted like it was time to race, Stjarna a sure loser.

I didn't get it, this was so unusual.

The sun was shining between puffy clouds that were lazily floating in the pale-blue sky. Racing to the pool, tearing off our clothes down to our underwear, we flung ourselves in. There was a big splash, and we shrieked gleefully as we jumped up and down in the naturally warm waterhole, which was the only geothermal heated hole in the area.

Hanna, being the adult, tried to slow us down without much success. The water was just right, and the four of us were having a glorious time. We'd been swimming for a good half an hour when the wind picked up, making us cringe every time we stuck our heads up out of the warm water.

Shivering, Unnur and Sína got out and wrapped themselves in towels. Gréta and I started to pull ourselves out when Unnur pointed to the water.

"Hanna is on the bottom, something is wrong with her!" She shrieked as she pointed.

I saw Hanna, face down, in the water. The way she looked I knew she wasn't pulling a prank, that wasn't like her anyway. Gréta and I dove down and got Hanna to the surface. She was deathly white and her wide-open eyes were totally blank. The braids had come loose and her golden hair floated about her face.

I screamed.

As in a nightmare, I heard Gréta yell.

"Sína, quick, ride up to the farm and get Jón! Unnur help us lift Hanna out!" But the dead weight was more than we could manage. We all were crying and sobbing, as we tried to keep Hanna's head out of the water until help arrived.

"I should have known something was wrong. It's my fault!" I wailed. "Thunder and Snati knew something was wrong. I should have known." My teeth chattered as I rocked back and forth, rubbing my eyes with my fists

"No, it wasn't anyone's fault." Jón, the farmer tried to comfort me. "I know Hanna's family and we've known she had heart problems since she was a baby. She didn't want to be treated differently than other kids. She wasn't expected to live much past her thirteenth birthday. This is very sad, but she lived her life the way she wanted to." He patted me on the shoulder.

The family came and took over. They tried to console us, but there was just too much to do. They asked Jón and his wife to take us to our respective homes. We got on our horses. Burying my face in Stjarna's mane, I sobbed my heart out. Unnur stared, dry-eyed, straight ahead. Sína and Gréta wept, tears streaming down their cheeks.

Jón and his wife rode back with us. At each farm, the couple quietly spoke with the families of the girls. Grandpa's farm was the last stop and Jón's horse galloped ahead. In one motion, he swung off his horse and dashed inside. Grandpa came running out, grabbed me off Stjarna and held me tight and whispered, "Hush now, it's going to be alright."

I stopped sobbing. I felt numb.

Björssi was standing by the door, stone-faced, as we came in.

He looked into my face. Suddenly he came to me and hugged me in a fierce hug before he bolted out the door. I heard Thunder's hoofs as he galloped away. [I didn't see Bjössi again. He'd moved away when I came back the following year. He married six years after this happened.]

"If we'd just not gone swimming, or if I'd listened to Thunder, maybe this wouldn't have happened. I knew something was wrong and I didn't do anything. It's my fault!" I stuttered.

"Come here, Diddamín" Grandma Sigríður wrapped her arms around me and led me to Grand-Amma who was in her rocking chair, lifting me up onto her lap.

"She was too young and pretty to die. I should have been able to save her." I started wailing again.

"Hush now, child. You heard what Jón said about her having heart problems since she was born. None of you, none of us, could have done anything to save her life. She's in Heaven now." Grand-Amma rubbed and patted my back, as she dabbed at her eyes with her hankie, then continued softly, "Hanna was doing what she wanted to do, be like all the other girls, as long as she could. You know she worked as hard, or harder, than many others, just to prove to herself she could. She'd like for you to remember how she enjoyed her life. She was a very happy, God-loving person. Remember how she had you put your hands together and had you repeat the prayer we taught you and your sisters 'Now I lay me down to sleep'… " I stopped her, putting my finger on her lip.

"Please, Grand-Amma, I don't want to hear the rest of it now." I whimpered.

The soothing rocking and her singsong murmuring relaxed me so that I began to think of Hanna. The more I thought, the more I remembered the way Hanna had lived and the numerous times she had mentioned God and His angels, even *guardian* angels, which I thought might be a very good thing to have.

I'd been so absorbed with my own life I'd not paid enough attention. I decided I'd like to be more like Hanna. I didn't know if I could do it. She was so good and I was... well...

For a change, for late August, it was almost warm outside. The four of us, Nonni, his two sisters, Sigga and Dóra and I were sitting halfway up on the turf-roof of the sheepcote.

"I'm going to miss you when you go back to Reykjavik next week," Dóra said, squinting at me with moist eyes.

"I'd like to go to school in the city." Nonni muttered, as he chewed on a blade of grass he'd stuck between his teeth.

Sigga didn't say a word. Her head was bent as she worked her fingers around a small tuft of grass.

"Well, I don't want to go. I like it here. I'd like to stay forever." I said, grumpily.

We sat for a while without speaking. I gazed over the farm, the ocean. On the horizon a ship was making its way north across the fjord, a plume of black smoke trailed in the air. It looked like a trawler and wasn't stopping at Vopnafjörður.

"I hope they had enough pins to protect Hanna." Nonni sat up, abruptly. "She was too nice to turn into a ghost."

I looked at him, stunned. Both girls turned their heads, mouths open, staring bug-eyed at their brother.

Nonni turned beet-red at our reaction.

"You all have heard the story, how you have to put pins into a dead person's shoes to help them from turning into ghosts." Nonni said defensively.

"Grand-Amma said that Hanna was in Heaven so she *couldn't* have turned into a ghost." I pointed my finger into his face so menacingly that he jerked his head back. "She also had a guardian angel to protect her. She didn't need pins. When I get older, I'm going to ask God for one of those angels. Maybe Hanna was so good because those angels kept her out of trouble!"

The girls nodded their heads agreeing with me, but Nonni looked troubled.

"Boys are supposed to be strong. I guess angels are alright to help girls, but I can take care of myself!" He looked at us defiantly as he stood up and brushed his pants.

I was going to miss my cousins.

Chapter 20

The North Fjords

Like an over-endowed, elderly, dowager elbowing herself through a crowd, the Gullfoss plowed through the ocean waves at a full roll toward Bakkaflói. The sky was lead-grey, the abominable stiff breeze bit my cheeks, and the gusts watered my eyes. The tip of my nose was red and ice cold.

Summer was over, and I was on my way back to Reykjavik.

I tucked my chin deep into the thick collar of my lopi sweater as I sat, hunched up, in the fo'castle amid coiled up brown rope and wood crates. I wrapped my arms tight around my chest as I rocked back and forth. Just a few hours of sailing and already I missed everyone at Vopnafjörður. I didn't want to leave. I didn't want to go back to Reykjavik.

A whiff of tobacco-smoke caused me to look up. Two men were standing by the rail. One of the men was round and short. The top of his head was covered with a black, limp hat. He had a curled-down, shiny black pipe clenched between his teeth. The pipe bobbed up and down as he spoke rapidly, both hands jammed into the pockets of his overcoat. The other was a taller, lanky, bareheaded younger man. With his heavy coat unbuttoned, he'd reached inside and looped his left thumb under one strip of his frayed, black suspenders, yanking and snapping as he used his straight pipe as a pointer. He would remove the pipe from his mouth with his right hand and jab it into the air as he made comments. The smoke odor reminded me of Grandpa and his attic. I squeezed my eyes hard.

"Are you alright?" I lifted my head at the concerned voice and felt a hand gently grip my shoulder. I looked up into the dark-brown eyes of Einar. He'd graduated from Iceland's Navigation School with my Father so I was quite comfortable with him "looking out" for me.

At age forty, he was two years older than my dad. His hair seemed to be of no particular color but he had lots of it; it stuck out from under his cap above his ears and curled at the neck of his black turtleneck sweater. Whereas Father was a stocky, short, solidly built man, Einar was tall, stoop shouldered and wiry. Both men had the strong, weather-beaten face of the seafaring man. Einar was a father of twins who were a year older than I was.

But right now I was wanting to talk to Sólveig, who had been so understanding as we traveled the fjords last Spring. Maybe she had answers for the questions that were churning inside of me. I knew she was going to meet the ship when we docked in Akureyri, and she just might be going back to Reykjavik. I was looking forward to that.

"Yes, thank you." I answered politely as Mother had repeatedly taught me.

"You're getting pretty wet from the spray. You look like a lamb that's fallen into a creek!" He chuckled as he brushed the water off my sweater.

Oh good grief, I thought. He sounds just like Sólveig!

"Why don't you go down below and dry off a bit? We'll be at the village of Bakkafjörður pretty soon." Looking up into his kind face, I nodded. Giving me a soft pat on the shoulder, he went back to work.

Clambering down the metal steps, I saw the back of a woman who slipped into a cabin. Something about the jet-black hair pulled into a tight bun looked familiar. I couldn't remember where I might have seen her before. I hadn't seen many passengers topside and wondered if they'd gone to bed already, or if it was because this ship was like a cork in a puddle. It rolled and wallowed in the smallest of waves.

The *Gullfoss*, built in 1915, was older than the *Goðafoss II* by six years. It was also somewhat smaller. The newer ship was 1,542 tons, whereas the *Gullfoss* was 1,414 tons. The ships were named after our better-known waterfalls.

I shared a cabin with three older, very quiet women. A top berth had rope webbing in front to keep me from rolling out of it when the ship tilted in a wave. The ladies took little notice of me, which suited me just fine. They seemed overly sensitive to the motion of the ship and had 'taken to their beds'. It got pretty raunchy-smelling in there at times, and I stayed topside as much as possible.

After changing into a dry sweater and pulling off my damp socks, I hung my wet clothes on a couple of pegs so they would dry out for another wear. By the time I came back up on deck, we were well into the bay of Bakkaflói. We did not go the dock, instead, a tugboat met us and loaded and unloaded what little cargo there was. No one got off.

I thought the small wharf looked dilapidated. The pilings were rotted in several places, high out of the water on one side and sagging low to the water on the other. I wasn't sure if the tugboat was running back and forth because the pier was unsafe or because of low tide. From the deck of the ship, the village of Bakkafjörður didn't look particularly interesting. Maybe the awesomeness of previous fjords had made me blasé.

Across the bay, Long Point was totally different. Stretching 40km northeast into the Atlantic Ocean, it ended in a pointy place called Fontur. As we sailed around the peninsula and looking at the forbidding faces of cliffs called Skóruvík my mouth dropped open, veritable millions and millions of seabirds filled the over-crowded sheer crags. It was mind-boggling. I couldn't imagine any birds left in the world. They must all be here on this rock-face! Stórikarl [Big Man], a rock column standing by itself in the ocean, was so teeming with Gannets it didn't seem possible to squeeze in another feather, let alone a whole bird!

The everlasting wind had become fairly calm, but felt bitter cold when I moved from a shelter. We were getting closer to the Arctic Circle. Sailing past these treacherous, amazing, sea cliffs, we came to another village named Þórshöfn, an old trading center. Þórshöfn means "Thor'sHarbor." According to Norse legend Þór was the thunder god and the son of Óðin, the most powerful of Viking gods. One night, Þór rode his eight-legged horse, Sleipnir, through the sky, at a flying pace. Sleipner touched one of his eight hoofs down on the ground, just west of Þórshöfn. To this day, his hoof print can be seen in an awesome rock-form as a giant horse-shoe. My mind went to Grandpa's attic and the Sagas. How I missed them.

I wrapped my sweater tighter and stared at the un-ending ocean as we sailed across the bay of Þistilfjörður and to the village of Raufarhöfn. While we were unloading the cargo, the town and the wharf became engulfed in a dense wall of fog, we had to stay moored longer than anticipated for fear of our ship ramming into another. But as often happened, stiff gusts moved over the restless sea and whipped away the fog. The *Gullfoss* was able and continued north.

At Hraunarhafnatángi, Iceland's northernmost tip, we started going west. The ship was sailing right along the Arctic Circle, less than a mile north of the peninsula.

On the north horizon, where open sea should have been, there appeared to be a huge land mass. In reality, it was massive, towering icebergs floating east and south in the North-Atlantic Ocean. It was far enough away to be of no danger to our ship, but the air got noticeably colder. As we continued west we encountered several ice-floes.

On one of the ice-slabs was a large Polar bear and another smaller one. This caused a terrific excitement and some fears among the passengers. I'd always thought that Polar bears were snow-white. But the larger bear was more straw-yellow than white. The fur looked bedraggled.

"They look sad and pitiful with their heads hanging down like that." One of the passengers remarked.

"They've probably traveled on that floe broken from those icebergs on the horizon." Einar said coming alongside where the group of us was gathered at the rail, watching the bears. "It'd be a shame if they try to swim to land. They'd be hunted down immediately." He shook his head, sadly.

"Why would anyone do that?" I exclaimed, appalled.

"There aren't any bears in our country and we want to keep it that way." Einar said, his voice husky. "A few, like those two, have drifted on ice close enough to swim ashore, but they were quickly disposed of. Folks here are extremely afraid of them and with good cause. Polar bears are very dangerous, especially when hungry." I was glad to see them float out of sight and hoped they'd find a place where they could be safe.

Chapter 21

Gunnar and the Polar Bear

In docking at Kópaskér, we were greeted by much excitement. Not just the kind as at previous villages; a hunt was on for a Polar bear sighted near the town. Folks were running and yelling. They were unable to agree as to where this animal was or even if there was one. A thirteen-year old boy named Gunnar Haldórsson had taken his rowboat out into the fjord to do some fishing. He had to navigate around an ice floe stuck half on shore and half in sea.

As he rowed his boat to the other side of the floe he saw something move on the ice, and then watched in horror as a bear, "bigger than my horse," jumped across the ice and loped up the countryside. With the hairs on the back of his neck standing straight up, he frantically rowed his boat back to the pier of Kópaskér, hollering and screaming at the top of his voice.

"Polar bear on land, I saw a Polar bear on land!"

Some men scoffed and made fun of him yelling for him to stop his nonsense.

"You probably saw a chunk of ice break off and imagined the rest." They hooted and took a swig of their fire-wine. But others took it seriously enough to follow Gunnar who showed them the bear tracks. That sobered up the doubters, and now many were arming themselves with any available weapons. Women and children were warned to stay indoors until the bear could be found.

On board the *Gullfoss* it was business as usual, but amid the loading and unloading, seamen were glancing over their shoulders checking out the activity of the villagers. The loud whooping of a group of men brought everyone to the rail. Some of us went off the ship and walked up to the knot of people that had gathered, jabbering and pointing.

"I'm not sure you should see this. It might be gruesome." Einar said as he and I followed the folks from the ship. Someone moved, and I saw what they were looking at. The huge bear was sprawled on the flat wagon, all four paws hanging over the edges. Bright red blood dripped from a hole in the middle of his broad chest. The small eyes were open, looking at me, lifeless.

All the agony of Hanna's death surged through my being. Trembling violently from head to toe I turned and ran toward the ship, nausea snaking through my stomach. I didn't make it. Halfway on the pier I had to run to the edge where I hung onto a reeking fish barrel. Sobbing and heaving, I vomited into the ocean, totally miserable.

Then I felt a cold, wet cloth on my face. Turning, I saw Einar's troubled face through my tear-blurred eyes.

"That was a magnificent bear, but very dangerous," he said. "It was obviously half starved and would have attacked livestock, or even people. The villagers had to kill him." Einar brushed my hair with his rough hands.

"I know," I gulped. "But it still doesn't seem right. None of this 'dying' stuff is right." I said, angrily. He looked at me puzzled. Reaching with his right hand he pulled me up to my feet, just as the whistle blew, preparing the ship for departure.

Dragging my feet, I went below to my cubbyhole of a bed. Tucking my knees up to my chin, I completely covered my head, twisting the blanket around me into a tight shroud.

Why do people have to drown? Why kill the poor bear? Then I remembered; I wanted Grandma to wring the rooster's neck, which would have killed him! Confused, I fell asleep.

Loud clamor, running feet and hollering jarred me awake. Peeking out the porthole, I jerked back as an enormous splash of seawater pummeled the glass. As I clambered up the metal steps, I heard thrilled voices of passengers squealing;

"There's another one! At least a dozen of them. Look!"

The astounding sight that met my eyes wiped out, for the time being, all my previous misery. The magnificent whales that breached gracefully, even playfully, up and down in the ocean were breathtaking. Their powerful spouts shot up like the Humpback whales south of Iceland, but these were much larger whales and their blowing were more forceful. Like the difference between Geyser and little Geyser their noise swooshed explosively into the air. I watched with breath-holding interest as we sailed across the wide bay of Öxarfjörður and into the bay of Skjálfandi where our next village-stop was.

Húsavik was an intriguing, picturesque fishing-whaling station. But I trembled at the thought of stopping here. I'd heard stories about men being shanghaied from this boisterous hamlet; rumor had it that captains from foreign whaling ships would ply Icelandic men with fire-wine and get them intoxicated. Then their sailors carried the unconscious men aboard their ships, thus replacing men lost due to illness, or having been thrown overboard for any perceived insubordination! I have no knowledge of this being true, but those telling it sounded believable.

Shuddering, and thinking this was one town I was not interested in exploring, I stayed on board and kept my eyes furtively glued on the comings and goings of foreign boats and their men. I saw nothing suspicious, and glad of it.

As we continued our journey, the sea was teeming with whales and seals. A killer whale shot up out of the ocean and seemed to do a slow twirl in the air. Its beautiful black and white body shone like it was dressed in a slinky, satin tuxedo. I was mesmerized and watched until most of the whales had swum north and out of sight. It was a good therapeutic feeling. I was back to enjoying the magnificence of the ocean and gazing at the hypnotic, and at times bizarre, coastline.

After we sailed past Flat Island I got real anxious and decided to go back below and check my clothes to see what I had to wear, wanting to look my best when I would see Sólveig again.

Chapter 22

Akureyri

We now entered the fjord of Eyjafjörður. As we sailed along the east coast, I could see the west side, as this is a very narrow firth. The mouth, where we entered, is the widest part of it being approximately 8 miles, but mostly, in its 20 miles length, the fjord is about 2-4 miles in width. On each side are towering mountains with steep hills that roll directly into the sea.

As we passed the island of Hrísey, I remembered reading the diary of Sveinn Þórarinsson "Hard Times in Eyjafjörður"*, an account of the dreadful times people had in May and June of 1869. The fjord was totally filled with ice and people were starving because the ships couldn't enter with supplies. At the end of this long fjord sits Akureyri, second largest town in Iceland. Hearing the *Gullfoss* announce our arrival with the usual blasts, I quickly finished changing my clothes and rushed back up. I found a place at the rail and leaned over staring hypnotically down at the seawatching the ships' wake. I'll never get tired of watching moving water, I thought.

More and more passengers were now gathered topside. Suitcases and boxes were piled close to the gate where the gangplank would be lowered. It was interesting to see how people dressed for the unpredictable weather. The older folks had only a sweater thrown casually over their shoulder or clutched in their hands. A few young men wore heavy coats, and had caps set at a rakish angle, while most of the girls were bareheaded, their hair blowing freely in the ever-present wind, and colorful lopi scarves wound casually around the neck.

Rain-grey clouds hung over the mountain tops, but the dock was dry. A sizable crowd had gathered to meet the *Gullfoss*. My eyes searched the group as they milled about. Then I spotted her standing to one side, shielding her eyes with her right hand as she watched the ship ease up to the pier.

She had thrown a large black shawl over her head. With her left hand, she bundled the scarf tightly under her chin. It made her look much older than she was and a little dowdy. But then she saw me waving and jumping up and down, and that wondrous smile of hers lit up her face and lifted my gloomy spirit.

"Have you seen this woman, Sólveig, your aunt told me about?" Einar had stopped. He carried a thick stack of papers in his left hand that he used to motion at the people on the dock.

"Yes, she's over there. See the lady right in front with the black shawl?" I pointed and waved, she waved back. Einar gave her a crisp salute.

"You'll have about three hours," he cautioned me." I'll check and make sure you get back, or your father will have my head!" His brown eyes twinkled, as he chuckled and walked away with the measured, purposeful steps so like my Dad's. I had a momentary sense of loss; I hadn't seen Father for many months. He'd been out to sea when I left last spring. I didn't see him very often.

I followed the folks that were now disembarking. Amid much shouting and greetings of the families meeting one another I worked my way to Sólveig. She had to take a few steps back as I exuberantly threw myself into her open arms. After hugging and laughing a bit we walked into town.

We seated ourselves in a small oceanfront café, a fancy word for the ramshackle, red-rusted corrugated shack that had five round scarred wood tables. A few chairs were scattered about in uneven numbers at the tables, as if people had indiscriminately used them and then not bothered to put them back properly.

In one corner, two men were playing chess oblivious to all but each other and the game. Four oil lamps were hanging from the rough, unfinished rafters, their chimney streaked with black soot. The place reeked of an odd mixture of fish, coffee, tobacco and kerosene.

We sipped on our coffee and nibbled at our cookies. Sólveig had already told me she wouldn't be going to Reykjavik at this time.

"The family needs me a little longer." She said patting my hand and looking into my gloomy face.

"The girls that I take care of are about your age," she continued. "I enjoy them very much. By the way, they are in Girl Scouts and last weekend I went with their group to Dettifoss and stopped at Lake Mývatn where they baked bread in the hot ground!" She rummaged a bit in the large black bag she'd carried. Then she pulled out a tin can and handed it to me. "I told them about our travel together so they baked this just for you."

"Tell them "thanks," I said. "I wish I could have been with them."

Baking bread in the boiling, geothermal mud holes at Mývatn how cool was that!

Pinching off a piece of the bread, I put it into my mouth rolling it around my tongue, tasting its sweetness. It was very good. Unconsciously crumbling a piece between my fingers, I dropped my head, staring at the crumbs on the table.

Feeling Sólveig watching me I looked up. Her eyes crinkled at the corners as she squinted at me with her eyebrows tightly knit, and eyes dark with concern. Her coffee forgotten, she leaned forward and reached out, laying her hands on top of mine she squeezed tight.

"This sad face of yours doesn't have much to do with me not going to Reykjavik, does it?" She asked.

I shook my head. "No. Well, maybe a little bit." My hands trembled in hers.

Sólveig nodded, waiting.

"Do you remember Íngi, at Seyðisfjörður and his ten-year old son, Ragnar, and the real bad storm we had?" I asked, pulling my hand away and rubbing my face.

"That's something I'll never forget." Sólveig shivered.

"Did you know they all drowned?" From the shock on her face, I knew she hadn't heard. Then I just spilled everything out about Hanna and ended up with the awful killing of the bear.

"So why did Ragnar, and his dad and uncles have to drown? Why did Hanna have to die? Even the bear hadn't hurt anybody. He was just hungry. It all seems so unfair!" I put my forehead down on Sólveig's hands. My eyes were dry. I couldn't cry anymore. I just wanted to understand. I'd been unable to talk about the things that lay so heavy on my heart. Events had moved too fast at Grandpa's and Aunt Þórbjörg's. The last Norwegian left the infirmary two days before I left Vopnafjörður. There seemed to be no time to sit down and really talk. I'm not sure I could have anyway so soon after the tragedy.

"I never saw such a girl for asking questions!" Sólveig shook her head, with a small smile.

Then she leaned forward, a serious look on her face.

"Listen, Íedamín, we know Íngi wasn't wise. Other fishermen had quit and sailed into the harbor for safety. Íngi had the same information on the weather as they had, but he chose not to heed the warning. Some people think they are invincible and nothing will happen to them. Many have lost their lives because of their own stubbornness. But also storms can come up suddenly and cause rogue waves and, through no fault of the fishermen, their lives may be lost."

She was silent for a moment, and then she bowed her head. When she looked up her eyes were misty with unshed tears.

"I met Hanna when she was thirteen." Sólveig said softly.

"I stared at her, startled. "You knew Hanna?"

"I met her at the hospital in Reykjavik, where my younger sister was a patient. They both had been born with heart problems and were not expected to live past twelve years of age. My sister died at age twelve. I was so glad to know that Hanna had several, wonderful, years. Her family writes me, and I knew how much she loved being with you and your family. Kind of funny. I didn't know the connection with you until just a week ago." She smiled at me.

Sólveig's story just completely lifted my spirit. It was really true, I couldn't have saved Hanna, no matter what I would have tried to do! I got off my chair and went to her, slipping my arms around her neck. All the guilty feelings rolled off of me. I felt light as a downy feather!

"Thank you Sólveig," I said. "I'm sorry about your sister, but she's in Heaven with Hanna. Isn't that just wonderful to think about?!" I kissed her cheek as she squeezed me tight, nodding her head. "And I really understood why the bear had to be killed. It would have been horrible if he'd gotten to a farm and killed people. I just overreacted... So will we meet in Reykjavik sometime?" I cocked my head giving her a big grin.

"Absolutely, elskamin!" She got up, grabbed me and whirled me right out the door.

The timing was perfect. The blast of the *Gullfoss* let us know my time was up.

Elskamin, my mind sang over and over as I ran up the

gangplank and boarded the ship. We'd already said our goodbyes, and Sólveig was walking away. I turned, just as she turned, and blew me a kiss. I felt on top of the world as I returned the kiss. I looked to the rest of my trip with eagerness instead of dread.

Clutching the bread tin tightly in my hand, I meandered to the bow of the ship. Scrunching down I wiggled until I was comfortable among coiled up ropes and some pieces of canvas. There always seemed to be plenty of thick rope, the size of my skinny arms, rolled up, fore and aft, making either place a cozy hide-away.

Opening the tin, I pinched off a lump of the dark rye bread and stuck it into my mouth. Contently chewing, I leaned back and stared up into the sky watching the clouds rolling and tumbling along. I loved clouds, and like the moving of water, they were an endless fascination for me.

Thinking about Sólveig's trip to Dettifoss - the most powerful waterfall in Europe - and the waterfall itself, I pinched off another piece of the bread and chomped away. It is not a pretty waterfall like so many others in our country, this one being fed from melting inland glaciers that always made its river muddy-grey looking. Grandpa had explained this when a group of us had gone there for a weekend. We had also stopped at the Krafla caldera, and the Víti crater. The Icelandic word "Víti" means "Hell." People often believed hell to be under volcanoes.

The bread was mouthwatering and I pinched off some more, rolling it in my mouth, I pondered the volcanic hot spots at Mývatn where the girls had been baking. I'd read how in the old days some folks had cooked their fish and mutton in the boiling hot water that bubbled out of the ground in various places on the island.

I wondered about other countries. Were they like Iceland?

Íeda Jónasdóttir Herman

Fire and ice side by side? Eerie looking lava-rock formations, deep crevasses slashed into the countryside? Boiling mud pools and steaming fumaroles? Volcanic eruptions and earthquakes every few years?

When I grow up, I want to explore what is beyond the endless horizon and find out, I thought to myself.

In 1965 and '67, American moon-landing astronauts used the Krafla and Askja area to study the geology for their lunar mission, as this barren lava field is one of the more moonlike places on earth. Krafla last erupted in 1984.

Chapter 23

The Herring Are Running!

As we sailed from Akureyri, we headed north in the fjord toward Siglufjörður. I thought about the tremor we'd had last year in Vopnafjörður that scared Lilla and me half to death. I knew the earthquake had originated near Dalvik, which is on the west side of this fjord and about halfway between Akureyri and Siglufjörður. I'd heard there was some damage in this area.* I craned my neck this way and that way, but wasn't able see any evidence from aboard the ship. The cliffs and rocks were just as high, just as formidable and bizarre as I remembered from previous journeys.

The grounds are always shifting in Iceland anyway. A volcano decides to explode and change the landscape. Some folks may go to bed at night then look out their window the next morning to see a new island forming practically under their nose, like Surtsey.

The island of Hrísey,* which is Iceland's second largest island - Heimaey being the largest, - sits in the middle of this long fjord, across from the Village of Dalvík.

As the *Gullfoss* plowed her way through the waves and past the island, a cloud of seabirds clamored in the air. I watched ducks fly up from the water and disappear among the clouds. The powerful ocean waves crashed and roared up the sides of the weird cliffs. I could, and did, spend hours upon hours watching the move of the restless sea.

As the ship eased up to the pier at Dalvík we passed a couple of boys sitting in their rowboat, fishing. They looked about my age. The boys waved and I waved back.

After the gangplank was lowered I disembarked and picked my way along the dock, around the, now familiar, coils of rope, barrels, and tubs of smelly fish. Men, both on-board ship and on the dock, talked loudly and shouted to one another as they worked at unloading and loading cargo.

Einar hollered something. I turned slowly and walked backward a step, then stumbled. Swinging my arm out I connected with a soft hand steadying me.

"Oops, careful there!" A woman chuckled. "I've got her Einar!" She hollered toward the *Gullfoss* where Einar stood by the rail. I lifted my hand in a wave to let him know I was all right.

"Well now, I guess introductions are in order." She smiled. "My name is Kristín Flósadóttir and I'm from Einar's hometown, Stykkishólmur." She was the small woman I'd seen disembark at Reyðarfjörður last Spring!

I wasn't surprised when she told me that she was a school teacher. I recalled that back then, when I first saw her, I had thought she looked like one. As we walked along on the pier, she proceeded to tell me that she was traveling back home and back to teaching, after hiking and exploring Gerpir.

"Nice meeting you, and thanks for catching me." I smiled, and politely stuck out my right hand. She grasped mine with a very small hand that was surprisingly strong. She had a big smile on her friendly face, and her dark, hazel eyes were fringed with the longest eyelashes I'd ever seen on a person. She wasn't pretty, but looked quite striking.

We walked about the village, as did most of the passengers. It felt good to walk on a surface that wasn't constantly moving under our feet. Several of us would thankfully stop for that ever-offered coffee and enjoy a moment of sitting at a table that sat on solid ground.

When I saw a couple of half-collapsed houses, I asked Kristín if she had heard about last year's earthquake here in Dalvík.

"We didn't hear much in Stykkishólmur. But captains and fishermen talk amongst themselves and I heard stories about how the quake caused gigantic waves to rise here in the fjord. A ship was tossed about in waves that men said were as 'tall as those mountains'."

Both of us gazed at the towering crags. I tried to imagine a wave of such monstrous proportion, but it was too mind-boggling. I couldn't wrap my head around it.

As we started ambling back to the ship, I saw the two boys still fishing. My mind went back to the story of the waves. Where were those boys last year when the monster-wave happened? I bet they were as scared as Lilla and I, even more so, being right here!

We sailed out of Dalvík and past a rock face scarred with great gullies. Cliffs with hues of grey, black, and slate-blue gave a spooky atmosphere to scatterings of stark, and lonely, farmhouses. They sat in tiny patches of sparse green grass in the barren mountainside that sheltered the 'picture perfect' harbor of Siglufjörður, one of the northern-most, and busiest [in 1935] fishing villages in Iceland.

Over a hundred fishing boats from numerous nations crowded the mountain-sheltered harbor. I tried to recognize the countries the flags represented but was able to name only ten or so. Kristín, the teacher, knew many more, but even she didn't know all of them.

The *Gullfoss* was still being unloaded when a great cry went up:

"*The herring are running, the herring are running.*"

The effect was electric. Boats were scrambling to race out,

each one trying to out-maneuver the other to get out as fast as they could and be the first to reach the enormous, silver- blanket of fish.

Way out in the mouth of the bay, we saw the wide band of silvery sloshing of herring stretching out into infinity. The heads of huge whales bobbed up, mouths wide open to gobble up millions of baby fish, while frantic seabirds screeched overhead and boats raced pell-mell into the melee.

Poor herring. Between man, whales and birds, they don't have a chance, I thought.

A sudden squall of rain caused Kristín and me to run for the ship. Passengers that were walking on the pier were getting dripping wet from the unexpected shower. The rain pinged noisily against the metal steps, rail, and smokestack of the ship. Then, just as quickly as it came, it quit. But the sky and ocean were turning an ugly, dark color.

The light was fading into gloomy grey by the time the crew had finished the loading of the cargo and we were back on our journey. The grey-black mass of clouds was dropping toward the sea with amazing speed. I could no longer see the activity of the fishing boats that, in so much excitement, had set out earlier. Lights bobbing up and down among the deep, dark waves was the only indication of boats in the area.

Suddenly, it seemed we were in a totally different world. The weather became horrible. Rain started pelting down hard, and at times, almost sideways. We'd sailed into the teeth of a gale coming from the direction of Greenland. The waves became huge. The hills of water towered higher and higher, and then rushed to meet us. The ship was lifted high into the air, and then went down, down, down, then up, up, up again. I wondered if it would just roll over and go down to the bottom of the sea. I thought of Ingi's boat and for a moment knew genuine stomach-gripping fear. What a terrible night to be out on the ocean.

Kristin had bid me goodnight and gone below. I was cowering under the steps that led to the pilothouse, out of the rain, as the wind rose to an unnerving shriek. I covered my ears with both hands as I followed the seamen with terrified eyes. Water streamed down their rain-hats and ran into their faces dripping into their beards. I watched them as they steadied themselves, firmly gripping cables and rail. Some were even grinning and just went about their usual activity. They are like my father, I thought, they love the sea, even as brutal as it can get. If they aren't scared I guess I don't have to be. But I really was. Dreadfully so.

I couldn't help but think of the "unsinkable" Titanic. Seamen still talked about the historic shipwreck that happened in April 1912. More than 1500 people drowned when the ship collided with an ocean-floating iceberg, now feared more than ever. I leaned forward, both hands clenched fiercely on my knees. Clamping my teeth, I muttered again and again, I won't be afraid, I won't be afraid!

I think I jumped a foot in the air when I felt a tap on my shoulder. I hadn't heard anyone coming. The noise from the howling wind and the smashing of the ocean against the ship drowned out everything else. The young man tapped my shoulder again and motioned up to the pilot's house where Einar was waving at me to come up. Swaying, and scrambling up the steps, the young man and I were drenched by the time we reached the door. The wind almost tore the door out of Einar's hand as he reached for me. I was glad to be with him, but the view from here was even fiercer than below.

At times, the ship was on top of waves that kind of eased out from under us, and the ship just dropped and came down with teeth jarring thump. The *Gullfoss* wallowed, plunged, and slopped seemingly in all direction but actually was making a sluggish, steady gain toward Hornbjarg peninsula. As the saying goes in Iceland, "Just wait a bit, this will change!" By morning, the weather did change.

We had sailed past Skagafjörður and Húnaflói while I slept through the night where Einar had securely tied me into a large chair. I was still snoozing in the warm pilothouse when the weather broke. He woke me up to see a magnificent sight; the sea cliffs rose steeply, dramatically, straight out of the ocean. A towering waterfall cascaded down the black lava cliff and plunged into the rocks and the seething, white-frothing ocean below. A few icebergs glittered on the horizon, while straggling calves bounced on the waves; heading wherever the wind would take them.

The captain, skillfully, steered the *Gullfoss,* skirting around treacherous the shore. We left the North Fjords behind and entered into the West Fjord of Ísafjarðardjúp and to the Village of Ísafjörður, our next stop.

* Hard Times in Eyjafjörður, appendix B
* Earthquake in Dalvík, appendix C

Chapter 24

The West Fjords

The northwest storm had pushed such massive ice from Greenland that all the fjords between Ísafjörður and Látrabjarg were packed with ice floes. Ísafjarðardjúp, through a quirky pattern of wind and waves, was spared this colossal intrusion. I was glad our ship had brought us safe through the, long, wicked storm.

What seemed like one hundred boats had taken shelter and were anchored about in the fjord. Two wooden piers ran out from the shore, the restless sea sending heavy waves sloshing up against its pilings. A, black and yellow painted, trawler and a small, red, fishing boat were moored to one pier, bouncing up and down with every billow.

The *Gullfoss* eased up to the other dock. Several people were gathered to greet us with the news that Dýrafjörður, Árnarfjörður, and Patreksfjörður, were packed with ice, and the passengers headed for those fjords would have to make a choice; either stay here and hope for the ice to break up soon, or to continue to Stykkishólmur and find a way back to their various destinations.

The crew had been unloading the cargo meant for this village. Upon learning that some passengers were staying (kind folks were coming down to the dock and offering places for them to stay), the crew then unloaded both personal belongings and cargo meant for the ice-blocked villages.

"Do you think that there'll be ice problems in

Breiðarfjörður?" I asked, turning to Kristín.

"I really don't think so. At Stykkishólmur we don't get near the ice these north fjords do." Kristín answered as she rubbed her chin and squinted her right eye, intently watching the animated knot of people gathered at the end of the pier. Motioning to the mountain across the bay, fingers were pointing, hands were wildly swinging. Women came and grabbed kids that were staring open-mouthed at the excited men. Voices were getting really loud and more men came running, yelling;

"WE'VE GOT TO GET THEM, NOW!"

Already, word was spreading like wildfire: A polar bear had come ashore. The men were acting like the so-called bloodthirsty Vikings of old, and the hunt was on...!

I, for one, was glad we were leaving. I had no desire to see more pandemonium over a bear. We were on our way out of the fjord when a young passenger, who looked to be about eighteen, came by the rail and stared intently toward the eastern shore.

"I thought I saw a polar bear going up toward Drángajökull." He muttered, as he removed his cap and scratched his head.

"Well, Bjarni. Why didn't you say something?" One of his friends exclaimed, disgusted. "We could've had some real fun watching the locals go berserk!"

Watching for a while, as we sailed past the mountains, we didn't see any sign of a bear. Kristin went below deck to do some reading and I was back in my favorite spot, crouching among the usual crates and large piles of coiled-up damp rope. A couple of old, yellow, life-rings with faded letters that spelled *Gullfoss* on them were propped up by the crates. I stuck my feet into the hole of one of them, and as my eyes scoured the horizon, my mind was back on the shipwreck of the *Titanic*. Seamen and passengers still talked about the "unsinkable" ship, even though it had been 23 years since the unthinkable tragedy took place.

I was looking out for icebergs and had every intention of shouting; *Icebergs ahead!* And thereby save the ship, and all the passengers!

We sailed out of the mouth of the fjord and turned west. As I looked north and west, the sea became a hazy undulating plain with no beginning and no end. I couldn't even see the faint outlines of Greenland.

When I grow up I'm going to see what's on the other side, I mused. Surely, women can be explorers. Many Viking women were written about in the Saga as being as brave and ferocious as the men. The problem was I was neither brave nor ferocious. I couldn't even stand up to the bullies at school!

The ship now turned south, and we sailed along the west coast of Iceland.

Jaw dropping, inky-black rock faces rose steeply out of the sea, meeting the stares of passengers that were gathered at the rail of the ship. Incredulous, I gaped at the home of millions of seabirds that were rarely disturbed, and left free to multiply into a chaotic horde. Now and then, a few hardy men would climb the spectacular sea-cliffs and gather eggs, or save seamen who had shipwrecked at the base of these perilous, hostile crags.

As we made our way around massive Látrabjarg, the western most land of Europe, I thought of the similarity of these cliffs, and the Skóruvik cliffs at Lánganes: One far east, one far west, both fascinating, fierce and menacing. Both peninsulas were notoriously treacherous to seamen. We made our way past these rugged coasts and entered Breiðafjörður, heading to Stykkishólmur, which is situated on the north side of a long peninsula called Snæfellsnes. This long arm reaches almost as far west in the Atlantic as Látrabjarg, but was far more hospitable.

The Gullfosswas now moving in soft rolls in a much quieter ocean; A nice change from the wicked weather we'd been through.

Although this was my fourth time to travel around Iceland, I had previously been either too young or too busy playing with my sisters, who had traveled with me, to pay much attention. Now, at the age of ten, and traveling by myself I was intrigued by this fjord. I was full of questions, curiosity and wild imagination!

Squirming, and making myself comfortable, I gazed across the bay, then turned over on my back and dreamily stared up into the cloudy sky and watched my favorite wild characters take shapes in the clouds as they moved and changed. A loud slap of an ocean swell against the hull startled me from my daydreaming. I sat up, stretched, and looked around. We were sailing slowly across the middle of this, very wide, fjord. I started thinking about the many tales I'd heard; how the, horribly greedy, ocean had claimed so many of mother's fishermen relatives in these waters.

I peered over the rail of the ship, down into the blue-green ocean waves slapping against the ship, as we moved across the fjord. I could imagine we were sailing over the bones of my forefathers. It was a gruesome thought.

My mother, Dagbjört Oktavía Bjarnadóttir, was born at Frakkanes and raised in Skorravík. Both are located on an inner peninsula in this fjord, across from Stykkishólmur.

Leifur Eiríkursson was born about four miles south of this area, at Eiríkursstaðir, the home that his father, Eirikur the Red, built and named.

According to Mother, Leifur is in our genealogy of ancestors.

The Saga records this story of the family; Eirikur had killed a man in Norway and was banished from the country, so he sailed for Iceland to cool off. Obviously, it didn't work; when Leifur was about twelve, his father, Eirikur, took him to Þingvellir, which is about 30 miles east of Reykjavík and was the place of the first parliament in the world. There, at *The Law Rock*, the chieftains and the people met annually. At the assembly, Eirikur got into a fight with a neighbor he'd been feuding with. He killed the man, and the Þing [Parliament] banished him from Iceland for three years.

He took his Long Boat, filled it with family and provisions, and crossed the Atlantic where he discovered an ice-covered island. In 982, when his banishment time was up, he sailed back to Iceland to tell people about this 'Greenland' he'd found. No doubt he named it so, to entice people to go with him and start a colony there. Surely Greenland sounds more appealing than Iceland, he must have reasoned.

Iceland has had several names. First one was Thule, or Ultima Thule, given by Pytheas, a Greek explorer in 330 B.C. The second name, Snæland (Snowland) was given by a Norseman Viking named Noddoddur, in 850.

The third name was given by Garðar Svavarsson, a humble Swede who named it after himself; Garðarshólmur [Garðar's little Island]!

Then came another Norwegian Viking, Flóki Vilgerðarson, who chose the name of Iceland, for the fjords were filled with ice, and the mountains covered with snow. He went back to Norway and bad-mouthed this inhospitable place. Later he changed his mind and came back and lived here for many years [12th Century Landnámabók; Book of Settlers]. The name 'Iceland' stuck. *

As the ship arrived at Stykkishólmur and maneuvered up to the dock, the passengers began to gather in little groups. Some were checking their bags and making plans on how to get to their various destinations. Others were loudly discussing the bears.

"Man, that bear I saw loping up the country side towards Drángajökull was huge! I thought at first that it was a white horse!" Said Bjarni, the young man, I'd seen back at Ísafjörður. He scratched his left ear and adjusted his brown stocking cap, pulling it down to his dark eyebrows.

"Maybe it *was* just a horse, Bjarni!" One of the guys howled in merriment, slapping his thighs.

"But a horse doesn't lope. I saw a *bear*!" Bjarni's voice was now adamant.

The young men began to holler over the side of the ship to a group of young women that were calling and waving.

"You should have seen...! Really, humongous Polar bears...!" Bjarni and his friend were whooping and shouting.

The bear story was getting bigger and bigger. Kristín and I grinned at each other, as we listened to the young men trying to outdo the other. It was getting pretty outrageous by the time the gangplank was down and the guys ran down to the pier to the group of girls. I can only imagine how many bears the story ended up having!

I didn't look around for Einar's family. He had told me that they were at their summer cabin at Kirkjufell for a few days, before school started. He gave Kristín a wave then went back to work.

I gave her a kiss on the cheek, and we hugged before she disembarked. She walked away with a firm step down to the end of the pier, where she called out to a group of young children teasing seagulls. When they saw her they started running and shouting, exuberantly throwing their arms around her. Two boys took her suitcases while other kids clung to her skirt. I wondered who they were. I'd somehow got the idea that she taught older students. I'll have to remember to ask her the next time we meet, I mused, as the group disappeared around a brown-rusted metal building.

And again the *Gullfoss* sailed on and went past the Snæfellsnes Peninsula where the glacier, Snæfelljökull, rose grandly to the sky. It is well known for being the setting for the novel "Journey to the Center of the Earth." A story written by the French author, Jules Verne, where he describes how a professor and his nephew hire an Icelander to be their guide in a daring exploration of the center of the earth, by entering a volcanic opening in Snæfell. The "Snorre Tarleson" in the story is based on Snorri Sturluson, author of Heimskringla, mentioned in the story by Verne.

As we continued sailing around Snæfellsnes Peninsula, toward Faxaflói, a wide bay we would cross to get to Reykjavik, I saw the tip of the glacier in the distance bathed in an orange glow from the just-below-the-horizon midnight sun. The sky was bathed in brilliant reds orange and golden glows making the clouds look like a fairyland.

Elves and 'Hidden Folks' are considered abundant in this area, and many farmers do not cut hay or disturb the ground around certain boulders. This was a well-known practice among farmers all over Iceland and not just here on Snæfellsnes.

A little over halfway in this fjord is Borgarfjörður. I mention that because one of our more famous ancestors Snorri Sturluson*, who lived from 1172-1241, had his home there called Reykholt. Snorri is also the author of Egils Saga one of the best known of the Icelandic Sagas. Grandma Sigríður is a direct descendant.

The sun was dangling a little higher on the horizon when we sailed between two urgently flashing lighthouses, and pulled into the harbor of Reykjavik.

Even though I hadn't wanted to leave Vopnafjörður, I was

getting excited at the thought of seeing my mother and siblings. Father was probably out at sea.

* I would like to mention again, that although the Vikings had a terrible reputation, cruel - blood-thirsty, etc. the truth is they were excellent sailors, ship-builders, craftsmen, daring explorers and great navigators who navigated by the sun and stars. They were also superb storytellers, rich in tradition that lives on in the Saga. And, for their times, they had a very open and democratic society.
* This is the same Snorri Sturluson mentioned in Verne's novel.

Chapter 25

Back Home in Reykjavík

Einar was now very busy. I'd thanked him already and said my goodbye. The hustle and bustle of the crew seemed to take much longer than usual. I guess that was not surprising, I thought; all the passengers would be getting off. It would be several hours before the ship would be scheduled to sail back out so the groups on the pier were folks waiting for the arrivals.

I was leaning at the rail with my two suitcases at my feet as I scanned the people, huddled in groups. I didn't see Mother, but then I spotted my Father. What a wonderful surprise. I was the first one to jump on the plank when it had been lowered. I flew down toward the pier and exuberantly flung myself into his arms.

Father gave a low chuckle as he tottered back and swung me around, and then put me down. "You have grown a little taller Íedamín, but still skinny as a rail!" Father grinned as he inspected me head to toe. "Trust you had a good trip. I heard from Einar that you had a few encounters with icebergs, and Polar bears." He brushed hair from my face and kissed me on the tip of my nose. Quite unusual, I felt a little apprehension.

"It's great to see you, Father. I was expecting Mother to meet the ship. Is she alright?" I tried to be casual, like this was nothing out of the ordinary. I turned as I heard a soft clearing of a throat behind me.

"Oh, thank you, Jón." Father took my suitcases out of the hands of the young seaman I'd seen working aboard the ship. I'd completely forgotten about them in my excitement at seeing Father.

"Your Mother is fine, so are your brothers and sisters." Father's voice was reassuring. "I'm meeting you because the *Gullfoss* arrived so early this morning, and my ship is docked just a couple of piers over." He pointed where an orange and black painted trawler was anchored. I knew Father was on another ship since the trawler he'd been on had shipwrecked last winter.

Derricks and cranes cluttered the wharf to the delight of the seagulls, and other seabirds that perched up high, their screeching piercing the quiet morning. Ships and fishing boats were moored at the pier. Another fifty or so were anchored in the bay, their various national flags hanging limply in the still air. A tugboat idly smoked near the entry of the harbor. I turned back and looked at the *Gullfoss,* mentally thanking her for bringing me safe through the awful storms.

The old tub did better than the fancy *Titanic!* Funny how one can get attached to ships that bring you safely home. *

We ambled toward the trawler. My Father, the ultimate seaman, was not tall in stature, he stood only 5'8" in his stocking feet. But he had an air of solid authority about him. His round, weather-beaten face was usually serious. Hooded dark-brown eyes, under dark heavy eyebrows made him look mysterious, I thought. He was wearing his dark-blue captain jacket and a white cap on his dark-brown hair. A tough, square-built man, without an ounce of fat, his body shaped and hardened by a hard taskmaster, the sea.

Father started walking with the slow-rolling gait of a sailor I always tried to imitate. I'd take a long step, then sway from side-to-side as if I were walking on a ship that was being pummeled on a high sea. This sent my two sisters into gales of laughter as they tried to imitate me, which usually ended in a squabble. I'd get fighting mad, run into a room and hide there with a book.

We walked along the base of one pier and passed a grey, weather-beaten, corrugated metal shed. The sea below was moving gently. In the rare stillness of the morning, I heard ducks murmuring. I peeked over the edge and saw them dipping their heads and paddling in formation under the wharf. An old skiff, broken and rotted-out, lay on the rocks of the shore, a perfect perch for the thousands of seabirds fluttering around.

We reached the second pier and turned to go toward the ship. A boy who looked about my age was sitting with his bare feet hanging over the rim of the dock, the legs of his trousers rolled up and over his bony knees.

A fishing-line, with a hook without bait, dangled from his hands. Three fish, a good two- feet-long each, wriggled in the hemp-bag lying by his side. His wrinkled red shirt was partly tucked into the waist of his pants. He'd pulled his black wool cap down to his almost-white eyebrows, and completely covered his hair.

"Good morning. Fish looks good." Father remarked as he touched the bag with his right toe. The boy turned, nodded his head and motioned for us to come closer. He pointed down to the ocean. We leaned over. It was unbelievable; all I saw were fish and more fish. They were in thick layers, flopping and sloshing over each other in the sea. The boy had literally dropped his fish line into the chaotic mess and pulled up his catch without bait!

Looking up, the boy grinned, his grey-blue eyes gleeful. "You know the saying, Cap'n, 'fish is food on the table and gold in the pocket.'" He said, chuckling.

"How right you are, son. How right you are." Father tipped his right hand to his cap and I waved at the boy when we heard a shout:

"Halló, Captain Jónas, breakfast is ready!" My Father was very well liked, and respected. Men addressed my Father as 'Captain', long before he was one.

"That's our cook, Juan. Are you hungry?" Father asked. I nodded as my stomach growled.

We walked up to the ship and I read the name *Max Pemberton**. An odd-looking, short man was leaning at the rail of the trawler, his black Kong-Fu mustache draped the lower half of his swarthy face. His black eyebrows went from the left of his brow, dipped over his nose, then continued to the right of his forehead. I was reminded of a black raven in flight. His dark eyes were piercing. Frankly, he scared the daylights out of me; he looked just like I imagined a pirate or a shanghier would look. But boy, could he cook! The table was loaded with cheese, boiled eggs, fish balls, dark bread, and hot coffee. He made coffee like no other; two dollops of export (chicory). My fears melted like ice in hot lava flow.

---

* Five years later, in 1940, during WWII, the *Gullfoss* was seized by Germans occupying Copenhagen, Denmark. Einar was not among the captives. By then he was on another ship.

* Father was with the skipper, Captain Pétur Maack, for several years then got his own ship. In 1944 the *Max Pemberton* disappeared in the Atlantic, never to be seen or heard from again. [Maritime Museum in Reykjavik, Iceland.]

Chapter 26

The "Look"

It was now the first week of September. Father had gone back out to sea, and it would be close to Christmas before we'd see him again.

We were all packed and ready to catch the old bus in the morning. Mother had planned for us to spend the week at our summerhouse and enjoy vacation time before school started next week. I wasn't to sure I'd be able to stand up to the bullies at school, but I knew I had to try Sigga's suggestion; to give their opinions to the trölls.

Our friends, Ása and Gógó (her name was Góa, but she stuttered and when she said her name it came out " Gó-Gó-Gó") had gone home after spending most of the day playing "hide and seek". It was late afternoon and Sisi, Lilla and I started to play hopscotch.

"Sísímín, I need for you to run down to the store and get milk to take with us in the morning." Mother stood in the doorway with the shiny, tin, milk-pail in her hand.

"Íeda, you go, I'm in the middle of this play," Sísí said and kept hopping. Tripping, she caught herself, barely touching the ground with her fingertips. "That doesn't count. I didn't put my whole hand down!" she yelled.

"Does too!" I screeched. "You go, Lilla. That's cheating, Sísí!"

"I don't want to. My turn is coming up!" Lilla hollered.

Mother gave each of us a searching look for a few seconds then, without a word, turned and went back inside.

"You know that's cheating, Sísí. You're not supposed to touch the ground. You lose your turn." I argued.

"My turn my turn... " Lilla started to hop at the beginning square. Sísí gave her a shove and my little sister promptly howled at the top of her lungs.

"That's not fair." We were all arguing and yelling at each other when Mother came out, purse in one hand and the pail in the other. She never said a word. I could hear Búddi and Frankel playing with their friends at the back of the house.

Sísí looked up as Mother started down the road. "I'll go." Mother didn't look at her.

My stomach churned. "No, I'll go." Terrible guilt built up inside of me.

"Mother, I'll go, I'll go." Lilla grabbed Mother's skirt. Mother kept walking, didn't look at any of us. She didn't look to the right or to the left but kept her eyes fixed on the road ahead of her. Her steps were long, solid and purposeful as she plodded down the street toward the milk-store. Mother was a small woman who now tromped her feet like someone twice her size. My guilt felt like a heavy rock in my stomach.

Sísí started crying, reaching out for the pail and pleading with Mother to let her go to the store.

"I'm sorry." She whimpered.

"Me, too." I sobbed as I scrambled after Sísí.

Lilla was crying and wiping her tears on Mother's skirt, barely able to keep her feet on the ground as she tried to keep up with Mother.

Mother kept clomping all the way to the store, totally silent.

Garður, the storeowner, looked up as we entered the shop, our faces dirty and streaked with tears, still begging. He inspected each of us, curiously. Then smiled into the calm face of my Mother who acted like she didn't know any of us. She didn't seem to be aware that we were around.

"Good evening, Dagbjört, what can I get you?"

"I need milk, Garður. I'm heading for the summer house in the morning."

"This is fresh milk and you have that ice-cold creek running close by your cabin to store the pail. That will keep the milk good for several days."

"I expect so." Mother nodded as she handed him the bucket. Garður took it from her hand and carefully filled the pail. Fastening the lid, he wiped off a small streak of milk dripping down on the side of the bucket, then handed it back to Mother who had taken money from her purse and laid it on the counter

"Do you need anything else, Dagbjört?" He glanced at us, standing by the door in a miserable heap, shuffling our feet and sniffling.

"No, thank you, Garður. The milk is all I need at this time. I'll see you when we get back."

"Thank you, Dagbjört. You have a good evening." Garður looked at us, opened his mouth to say something, but when he saw Mother's set face, he clamped his teeth and eyed us soberly.

Quietly reaching over Lilla's head, mother pushed the door open and stepped out. She didn't look at us but started walking the same way, all the way back home.

Mother was a very easy-going good-natured mother who never yelled at us. We were never spanked, but there were times (like this time) when I'd rather have the spanking than the "look" and the silent treatment.

We sniveled all the way home. The three of us never forgot.

I must have driven my mother to the edge of her patience with my insatiable reading. One day she came into our bedroom where I was curled up on the floor beneath the window, totally absorbed in a book. Taking it out of my hands and gently, but firmly she said; "It's your turn to clean your kids' room. Sísí did it the last time. I'll give you the book back when you're through." With my book in her hand, she turned at the door and gave me *"that look"* then walked out of the room and closed the door.

Half-heartedly, I started picking up clothes and putting them away. I glanced around and saw a corner of a book sticking out from under a pile of socks. Now, mind you, I wasn't going to read it; just see which one it was, just the title you know...

"I thought I removed all the books!" Mother's voice was inches away from my ear. I must have jumped a foot high into the air. It was getting to be a habit! I'd get so engrossed in day-dreaming or reading I'd forget where I was or even what day it was.

I watched sheepishly as mother hunted for more books that might be hidden. Turning to me with a deep frown between her normally twinkling blue eyes, "Couple of women are coming over and I want you to have these clothes folded up and put away by the time they arrive. That will give you one hour. Is that clear?" Mother's firm voice was very clear. I nodded.

I did quite well once I got going. The clothes were put away and the top of the duvet was smooth. I finished by dusting the top of our chest of drawers and then sweeping the floor. Putting the broom by the door I sat back down on the floor by the window, the best light for reading. Looking around I made sure I hadn't missed anything. Twisting my fingers and twiddling my thumbs, I sighed. No books.

Scratching my head I straightened out my leg and wiggled the bottom duvet with my toe, a smidgen of paper slithered out. Eagerly I picked it up. It was one page that was missing from one of the books mother had removed from the room. I was totally in another world when I heard the explosive laughter from mother and her friends as one of them exclaimed, "Just one piece of paper, she is hopeless, Dagbjört!"

But the room was as neat as when Sísí cleaned, and I got my books back!

Chapter 27

Mother Falls into Volcanic Crevasse

We were at the summerhouse enjoying our vacation; fishing, splashing in the creek, and skipping stones, when the wind died down enough for the water to be still. It was quite a competition among us to see how many times a rock would skip and hop before sinking.

Other times we'd find small lava rocks that would float. This fascinated Frankel the most, he looked under the pumice to see what made it move.

"There should be a motor." He fussed. We showed him how to throw pebbles to cause waves in the water so he could see his little 'boat' wobble and bobble. I picked up a stick and stirred the water some more.

"See, that's how the Vikings looked at the current," I said. "They didn't have a motor on their longboats, only oars. They studied the waves to see which way to go for their discoveries." This made Frankel very content, he liked to hear the stories about the Vikings, as we all did. He could lay on his stomach for hours and watch the 'Viking boat' move.

The widest part of the creek that ran across the field in front of the little house was pond-like, and shone like a mirror on this particular afternoon. The fish plopped up and down, pink and silver scales shining in the elusive sun. Wispy, raggedy clouds hung in the grey-blue sky. A group of seagulls hip-hopped on the rail of the wood bridge that spanned the creek. Cocking their heads and puffing up their wings, they watched the fish jump in and out of the water.

This, our last day, was unusually still and mild. The mountain range was hidden in soft, lazily floating, grey-white fog.

Iceland's most wicked volcano, Hekla, sat quietly in the distance, her usual, perpetual, white fluff hanging over her in the sky.

Mother's summerhouse was in the country at a place called Laugberg a short drive from Reykjavik. The only other house, barely in sight, was a farm across the creek, sitting a way up in the countryside. We kids called them "the rich people" because their farm was so large. The farmer there raised pigs and was looked down on with much disdain by the sheep farmers.

Our cabin was a small two-room place, divided crosswise in the middle. Two bedrooms were in the back part. Built-in beds lined two walls in each room. Each bed had its top and bottom down-duvets. The bottom duvet was the only kind of 'mattress' we had.

The sitting, dining and cooking area was in the front part of the cabin. Pots and pans were stacked on open shelves by the black, peat-burning stove. Dishes, cups and saucers were on shelves built on each side of the center-placed bare window. The dishes would clatter and dance noisily at the smallest earth-tremor. A wood table with six chairs placed two to a side and one at each end sat in front of this window.

On the table were four wood cylinders ornately carved with old-time scroll-pattern, and the words; *Hnífar-Gafflar-Matskeiðar-Teskeiðar (Knives-Forks- Soupspoons-Teaspoons)* each one filled with the appropriate utensil.

A roughly built, long bench served as a sofa, where plump, eider-down-filled pillows of various sizes in red, brown and white and a few fur ones, were propped haphazardly up against the wall. A rough, wooden ladder was in one corner, it lead to a crawl-around-only attic. The three of us girls would sleep up there when, Gróa, or a visitor came to stay overnight.

Lilla and I were sitting outside on the top step. We were finishing a long necklace that we were making from the dandelions we'd picked. Snipping off the yellow blooms, we made a circle out of the stems by threading the ends together then looping each one to make a chain. We'd made a bracelet, a coronet and a necklace that now decorated Lilla. We were working on more necklaces for Sisi and me, and hoping we'd have enough to finish, as the weed was getting scarce.

"Do you have the scissors?" Lilla asked, running her hand under the pile of dandelion heads.

"No, I don't have them. Maybe you're sitting on them, or maybe the 'Hidden Folks' needed to borrow them." I searched half-heartedly around me. "If they borrowed them, you know the scissors will turn up. The 'Folks' always return stuff."

Scowling, Lilla stood up.

All of a sudden, horrendous screaming and crying echoed through the air. As we jumped up and ran down the steps, we saw Sísí coming across the lava field. She had her skirt hiked high up with both hands so she could run faster.

She stumbled and cried when we reached her. I couldn't make anything out of her stuttering, but I saw Frankel sitting on the ground mouth wide open crying, "Mamma, mamma!" Búddi was on his stomach, both arms flailing, feet kicking in the air. He was looking into what seemed to be a narrow split in the moss-covered ground.

"What happened to Mamma!" Lilla cried.

"She fell into a crack in the ground. I thought I heard her cry, but now she's awful quiet." Sísí finally gulped, tear streaming down her cheeks.

"We'll have to get help from the pig-farmer!" I turned to Sisi, who was wiping her face with her skirt.

"I'll get him. Sisi, you're the oldest you have to stay with Mamma, and the kids." I started running for the creek.

"Don't you dare!" Both of my sisters screamed.

I stopped, turned, and stared at them.

"What else can we do? They are the only people close by. We've got to get help!" My stomach was in knots. I had no idea how badly Mother might be hurt, but I knew I couldn't waste time. The lava rocks are sharp and can cut deep, and Sísí had indicated that Mother was unconscious. I turned and ran towards the distant farm and started to cross the ice-cold creek. Wadding my skirt into a knot, I stomped into the rushing water that came up to my knees.

I saw the young roan just on the other side of the bank.

"You're gonna get killed." Lilla shrieked. "Remember the last time!"

Oh yes, I remembered the last time. I had disobeyed and gone across this same creek and jumped on this same colt. He had promptly bucked me off his back and knocked me out cold. I had promised, "cross my heart" never to go over that creek again! But this was an emergency I assured myself.

Carefully, I crawled up the bank on the other side. This time I wasn't going to surprise the horse. I talked to him, my teeth chattering.

I took a running leap and jumped onto his back. Snorting fiercely and shaking his head, he took off like he'd been whacked on the rump. I was ready. I fastened my legs tightly to his smooth back and clenched both of my fists into his air-tossing mane as he galloped toward the farmhouse.

As we neared the huge pigpen, the farmer came running

Íeda Jónasdóttir Herman

toward us, purple-faced, and both fists angrily pounding the air. Then, leaping, he grabbed his horse by the neck and quickly brought him to a halt as he growled at me.

"I told you the last time if you ever... !" He stopped as he saw my terrified, tear-streaked face.

"All right, girl. Don't look so scared. I'm not going to hurt you, but you really . .." He scowled.

"It's Ma...ma" I stammered as I slid to the ground, tears pouring down my face.

It was surprising how gentle this 'horrible, bad-tempered pig farmer' became. I was terribly afraid of him. He was known to have a short fuse because people gave him a hard time over raising pigs, nasty animals that looked gross and smelled worse. The sheep farmers around here argued 'No one that had any sense would eat such meat! They were as unclean as chickens that no one eats. But at least chickens laid eggs and had useful feathers!'

Patting my head, he turned, whistled for his older horse, which promptly came running, and then he roared. "Helga, come here!"

"Coming, Árni." The woman turned from the clothesline where she'd been pinning snow-white sheets. The snapping sound of wet cloths followed her as she slowly plodded closer to us. Then she stopped.

Furious, she knit her black heavy brows, and grimly fastened her gimlet eyes on me. She was large of bone and feature, and looked very strong. I was scared to death of her, too, even when she didn't look so grim. Firmly, she placed her hands on her ample hips and glared.

"You really are in trouble now. I've got a good mind to... "

"Hold it, Helga." Árni waved his right hand. "We have an emergency. Her mother is hurt. Get your first-aid kit and come on over. I'll go now and take the child with me. I'm amazed she was able to hold onto this unbroken colt." Árni was putting the reins on his horse as he talked. Swinging his right foot over the horse's back, riding bare-back, he moved and made room for me in front of him. Then he reached down as I lifted up my hands.

Árni gave his horse a smart whack and we went at a brisk gallop across the lava-field, sloshed across the creek where Lilla and Búddi were waiting, faces wet and streaky from tears. Sísí was holding Frankel, rocking and crooning.

She looked up as we rode up. Árni lifted me off after he had dismounted, and I ran to Sísí. All of the kids were trying to talk at the same time.

"Mother is alright. She can talk, but she hurts." They babbled, as Árni knelt down and looked into the crevasse.

"Halló, Dagbjört. Talk to me." He said." How are you hurt? Can you move at all?"

There was noticeable relief in Mother's voice as she gasped, "I'm alright, Árni, but I can't move my right ankle without hurting pretty bad."

"Helga is riding up now. She'll come down and look at your foot. We'll get you out of there pretty soon." Árni's voice was reassuring.

Helga was riding up at a flying pace. She had tied her skirt up between her legs so she appeared to be wearing black, billowy, bloomers making for easier bareback riding. Interesting design I thought. I was impressed. In one surprisingly fluid motion she was off the horse and kneeling down by her husband.

Lilla and I had climbed on top of a boulder so we'd be out of the way. Búddi and Frankel sat on the moss below our feet, while Sísí stood by Árni, ready to help.

Helga carefully scrambled down into the hole. We could hear the murmur of her voice as she spoke to Mother.

"No broken bones, Árni." She called, "I'll wrap her ankle so we can move her. But first, hand me your bottle. We'd better give her a stiff drink." As he handed her the bottle we heard the two women giggling like a couple of young girls. Then her hand came up, something seemed to be wadded up in it.

"Look here, Árni, our little Kisa was down here, I didn't know she had wandered off!" She lifted a small, coal-black, mewling fur ball to her husband. He gently stroked the small head with his big hands then handed it to Frankel who seemed in awe of the purring creature. We never owned pets.

After careful lifting and pulling, the couple were able to get Mother out. The fissure was only about six feet long, three feet wide and five feet deep but had sharp, jagged cinder rocks on the bottom. Mother had landed on the side of her right foot, hitting her head on the edge of the rift as she fell in. She had a large bump on the back of her head.

Helga had wrapped Mother's right foot from toe to knee. I couldn't imagine how anyone could jam so much bandage into such a small emergency kit.

"I feel like a silly sheep, falling in like that. I thought I heard a child cry, but it was the kitten. I could feel the brittle shale giving way at the edge, but I couldn't stop my falling." Mother shook her head, then groaned and grabbed her head in her hands, then, looking up she saw Lilla and me sitting on top of the rock.

"Sísímín, get the girls off of there. They know better." She murmured.

Lilla and I looked at each as we scurried down. Yes indeed, we knew better. She had told us numerous times not to climb on that particular rock.

"Remember your cousin who limps? She got that way because she climbed a huge rock that was known to be a castle of the elves. They don't take kindly to kids who climb on top of their buildings." She had warned us.

Fearful, I looked behind me as we followed Sísí, who had Frankel and Búddi by a hand. Frankel had the kitten wrapped up in his sweater, protecting the bundle with his free hand. I didn't see the angry elves, but I walked a little faster, dragging Lilla with me.

Árni and Helga crossed their hands together and formed a seat for Mother to sit. She wrapped her arms over the neck of each of them, and we all walked slowly toward the cabin to wait for Gróa. The farm couple had offered to stay with us, but Mother assured them that we'd be alright. Nanny Gróa would be on the evening bus as planned, as she was coming to help close up the cabin for the winter.

Mother thanked them for their kindness and we kids stepped outside to wave as they rode off.

I thought of the kind way they treated Mother, and even me, although I had caused them trouble. I hoped I'd never listen to other people's opinion about folks.

Frankel's lower lip quivered as he watched the kitten curl up in front of Árni. Mother had told the kind couple that we couldn't own a pet, when they offered to give it to Frankel. He was a quiet boy who liked to play by himself. He loved trucks - machines of all kinds fascinated him. He would use sticks and rocks for his imaginary trucks and make roaring noises as he 'drove' his machines up and down the plank-walls of the cabin. He'd grown rather independent during the summer I'd been gone, which was a good thing since Búddi was so rambunctious!

Sísí herded us back inside and got us started on packing our own stuff.

Later, Búddi, Lilla and I stood by the side of the road and watched the rattling bus lumber up the volcanic-cinder, one-lane road. Gróa got off, and immediately we all started talking at the same time.

"Mother fell into a crevasse... " I started.

"She hurt her head and foot... " Lilla hopped around Gróa.

"The pig-farmer and his wife came... " Búddi said, excitedly.

"Whoa, hold it. One at a time." Gróa stopped. "Your Mother is all right?"

We all vigorously nodded and followed Gróa inside.

The next morning the weather had changed. Hard, northeast gale was blowing across the lava field. Dark-gray clouds scudded across the somber sky.

We kids and Nanny Gróa were bundled up in lopi sweaters and knit caps as we sat by the road, suitcases by our feet. We heard the rattling old bus drive up the ash covered road. All of us jumped up as it swung up to our lane and stopped.

Gróa talked to Skúli, the bus driver, for a minute. Then both of them walked up to the cabin and went inside. Pretty soon they came out carrying a bundled-up Mother the same way as Árni and Helga had done; clasping their hands to form a seat, as Mother wrapped an arm around each one's neck.

Walking down the lane and over the wood bridge was a good distance and both Gróa and Skúli were puffing hard, as they reached the bus. By the time Mother was settled in, and the pillows we'd brought out were cushioned under her foot, she looked very pale.

Just three days and we'd be back in school. I dreaded it.

Chapter 28

Óli the Bully

Gógó and I stomped grumpily down the crowded, blue-painted hallway that smelled strongly of green lye-soap. Neither one of us were happy to be back in school where both of us were teased unmercifully, I, because of my name and Gógó because she stuttered.

We entered the classroom where Óli and his two friends were already seated. My heart sank. I was destined to put up with those hooligans forever. And to make matters worse, my desk was in front of Óli's, giving him perfect opportunity to annoy me, yank my hair, and whisper taunts, without being detected by the teacher. Gnawing at my lower lip my face felt red-hot as my temper rose ten degrees.

"Good morning, children. My name is Ínga and I'll be your teacher this year." The teacher was disgustingly cheerful as she swung a blue and white-checkered towel over her shoulder. On her left arm hung a small tin bucket, and in the hand she had a bottle full of a shimmering, sickly-yellow, oily liquid. She had a large tablespoon in her right hand that she jabbed in the air as she spoke.

"You know the routine of first things first." She chuckled as if she were enjoying a huge joke.

I brushed strands of hair from my face and looked at Gógó who was sitting at the desk in front of me. I could see the red flush creep across the back of her neck, blending with her red hair. Slowly she turned, we rolled our eyes at each other; the cod-liver oil! My mouth went dry. Desperately I tried to think of some way to get out of having to take the oil...

"Hold your nose and open wide, Góa." Teacher's voice was positively chirping!

How can she be so chipper? She knows we all hate this stuff. I was sure I was going to throw up in front of all these kids. Óli and his friends would never let up on the teasing and name-calling. I'd never be able to come back, or maybe I'd be lucky and just choke on the stuff and die on the spot! I grit my teeth.

Then I thought, if I keep gritting my teeth it'll be my luck to be toothless, like old Olga. Unconsciously I snapped my fingers like I'd been practicing for so long. All of a sudden, I relaxed. I bit the inside of my lip to keep from giggling. I'd forgotten Sigga's advice on the bullies! I sat up straight in my seat as Ínga stood by my desk and happily sang out;

"Hold your nose and open wide, Íeda."

"Íeda... " I heard Óli snicker behind me.

I turned to him and hissed, "I gave your name calling to the trölls." I smiled sweetly at the teacher, who was looking at Óli, her smile replaced by a tight frown knit between her green eyes.

I pinched my nose with the thumb and fingers of my right hand and opened my mouth wide, for the teacher to pour in a spoonful of the stomach-churning stuff. With heroic effort, I managed to nonchalantly swallow. She nodded her head a couple of times then turned to Óli.

"Your turn, Óli. Hold your... "

"That's girl stuff. I don't need to hold my nose." Óli boasted.

The spoon clicked against his teeth as Ínga poured the yellow liquid into his mouth.

"Swallow!" The teacher was firm, no longer cheerful.

I heard Óli's strangled gulp and turned just in time to see him turn grey-green, gag violently, and then throw up into the bucket Ínga was holding. With a wicked smirk on my face, I leered into the red face of my tormentor and snapped my fingers. My antagonist's eyes glared at me.

The first day was always the hardest. After that we were okay with the routine of the 'first things first' dose of cod-liver oil. I never gave it a thought that this wasn't the most hygienic way to administer the potion, but the cod-liver oil sure kept us healthy!

After three weeks of unusual autumn days where we had been able to enjoy the out of doors, the weather took a nasty turn. Rain turned to sleet, and Mt. Esja was covered in white from her top down to the seashore. Rime covered the walkway to the school, and icicles hung from the metal pipes that formed a handrail.

I got my, regrettable, second revenge.

Sísí, Lilla, my friend Gógó and I had arrived at school all bundled up. We, carefully, walked up the icy steps as Óli and two of his buddies gleefully kept their eyes on us. A metal flagpole was fastened at a slant to the iron rail. The Icelandic flag hung limply in the sleet. Óli had perched himself up on the rail and grabbed the pole with his, bare, left hand.

"Gógógógó... Íeda... " They started their taunting.

"Get your hand off of there, Óli!" Ínga's voice was shrill with alarm. She'd just stepped out to ring her school bell.

Startled, Óli slid down and slipped, still holding the pole. His hand was stuck. His face swung against the pole. He opened his mouth to yell, but all he could do was grunt. His eyes were bulging in terror. The tip of his tongue was frozen to the iron flagpole!

Other teachers came running when we all started screaming. Ínga was telling Óli not to move as she held his head tight to her chest. Boiling hot water was brought out and poured on the pole. In a short time, Óli was free. His left palm was sore for a few days and it was awhile before he was able to speak or eat properly. I behaved, I didn't sneer at all. The truth is, I felt sorry for Óli, and the whole episode was rather traumatic for all of us.

I can't say that I remember the teasing easing up a whole lot, but I do remember that from then on I didn't let it get to me like I used to. Perhaps it was because Mother started tutoring me a bit in the catechism of the Lutheran Church, dwelling quite a bit, I thought, on forgiveness.

Although Icelandic children are confirmed at age 14 and I was just going on eleven years of age, I guess I needed more time to get rid of my heathen ways and rid myself of the belief in this 'silly superstition of trölls and Hidden Folks.' It was easier to quit believing in trölls and ghosts than hidden folks, after all we were being taught in church that 'many had entertained angels unaware.'

I thought that meant they were invisible and therefore 'hidden.'

Chapter 29

Christmas 1935

Of at least 27 public holidays observed in Iceland, our family celebrated only Christmas, New Year Eve, Easter, Bolludaginn (Bun Day), Ash Wednesday and Easter.

We didn't make anything of birthdays, never celebrating any of them.

I vividly remember the Christmas of '35, probably because it was so unusual for Father to be home.

Father had arrived back home after a fishing trip to England. He was quieter than usual and speaking with Mother in a hushed voice about a war in Europe. I didn't pay much attention thinking that was far away and wouldn't affect our small isolated island. Right now, we were as excited as could be; Father was taking us to a Seamen's Christmas Party held at the Opera House.

Our water line had frozen, but Gróa got a dishpan full of snow and melted it so we could to wash up. She took care of the boys while we girls washed ourselves, with Mother's supervision. Then she brushed our hair and had us turn a few times to make sure we were presentable. We girls wore our Icelandic dress-ups - ornately embroidered with gold thread, red vest over a white blouse, black skirt and tasseled cap on our head. The boys wore green jackets; their short breeches were tucked into their long socks just below the knees.

Bundled up against the winter blast until we looked like overstuffed sausages, we waddled downstairs to a waiting, decrepit taxicab that Father had so extravagantly called for.

All the church bells in the capital of Reykjavik were chiming at the same time, the Dómkirkjan [Lutheran Church, Iceland's state church] in down-town Reykjavik, the Catholic Church sitting high on a hill, and the Fríkirkjan [The Free Church], down by the lake, all were ushering the start of the Christmas Season. Our holiday started promptly at 6:00 PM on the 24th of December. The loud ringing of the bells added to the festive air.

The dark-blue sky was lit up with, pinkish-green, shimmering curtains of rapidly moving lights. The Aurora Borealis [Northern-lights] were in full display of red, gold, and purple streaks as the brilliant colors shot across the sky in a breathtaking show. Up and down, side-to-side the lights danced across the heavens. We kids craned our necks this way and that, pointing, *ooh-ing* and *ahh-ing* over each wonder.

In much excitement, we kids erupted out of the cab and into the entry of the Opera House. Father stopped to greet someone as Mother continued inside with us kids. Suddenly we stopped: The giant Christmas tree at the party was awesome, its top reached clear up to the vaulted ceiling. The few trees we had in Iceland didn't grow to such massive height. I knew it had to come on one of the ships from some far-off country.

I threw my head way back to try to see the top. The hundreds of lighted candles flickered in the huge ballroom. Red, green, yellow and white paper-chains were wrapped around and around, from top to bottom. Various sized and intricately shaped bags were hanging from the branches, each bag bulging to overflowing with hard candy!

Rollicking accordion, and violin, music reverberated through the air. The place was already filled with children and their parents. We stood mesmerized, rooted to the wood floor that we could feel shaking, and crackling, like aftershocks of an earthquake. The kids had formed a circle and were hopping, clomping, and swinging in a dance around the tree. Sisi, Lilla and I grabbed hands that reached out to us as kids twirled by. Even Búddi joined the fun. But Frankel couldn't stop staring at the tree. He stumbled and tottered around, blue eyes scrunched half-shut, as he followed Mother.

"What's the matter with your eyes? Why are you closing them like that?" She was getting concerned.

Frankel was like one hypnotized.

"When I squeeze my eyes it makes hundreds and hundreds of lights, maybe millions, maybe gazillion trillion lights!" Not until the candy bags and oranges were handed out did Frankel quit his squinting.

We were a happy, but tired bunch that went home that night, chattering in excitement what tomorrow was going to bring.

We woke up Christmas morning with the kitchen sending out an aroma of cardamom, cinnamon, and vanilla. Gróa was baking twist-cookies and pancakes. She'd spread the center of the pancakes with jam and topped them with dollop of whipped cream. Mother folded a cake in half and again in half, so it looked like a triangle. We needed forks to eat this rich, yummy treat.

After we had eaten and Gróa was clearing the table Father told Mother to have us sit down and wait, then he quickly disappeared into the bedroom.

My toes tingled in anticipation. We'd never had store-bought toys, but we always got something carved or knitted, just for us, and sometimes we had an orange each. We'd put the orange-peel in a glass of water with a spoonful of sugar and let it sit overnight. That was our next morning orange juice!

Father came out with his arms loaded with boxes, full of stuff from his trip to England. We started jumping as Búddi was handed a truck. He seemed speechless for a change. Then he whooped and fell to the floor with the truck. When Frankel got his, he inspected it from end to end, looked under it, and turned to Mother with his eyes sparkling.

"This is the biggest and the best." He breathed.

We, girls, each got an almost, life-size, plastic baby-doll. This Christmas was beyond our wildest dreams!

A few days later, Búddi was in the kitchen by himself. I heard him muttering. I crept closer. I was going to jump at him and scream just to scare him.

"Are you scared yet?" He asked.

I crept closer. Who is he talking to? I wondered, as I snuck up to the door and tiptoed up behind him. He had a lighted candle in his hand and was holding it close to the nose of my doll. I could feel my eyes widen, ready to pop out of my head!

"Are you scared yet?" He bent closer as I opened my mouth to scream.

Suddenly, there was a sound of a hissing sizzle, then *pouf!* My plastic baby-doll disappeared, like a genie out of a bottle!

Shocked, my mouth still open. No sound came out of my throat. I stared at this tiny, weird-shaped, pink blob that had been my beloved Christmas present, then into the bulging eyes and white face of my brother, who slowly sank to his knees, then lay flat on the floor, unconscious.

That's when I started screaming. My doll was dead and I thought my brother was dead, too.

I don't remember getting another play doll. But later I was given a doll dressed in a black, ornately embroidered with gold thread, Icelandic National dress. She had long, curly brown hair on her china head. Her hands, and feet were also made of china.

The cloth body was stuffed with cotton. For along time, the doll sat on a high shelf among my books.

A couple of days later Búddi was fine and so was I. Another adventure was already scheduled and our minds were now on the New Year's Eve festivities and New Year's Day Dinner.

The group of us kids, with Mother and Gróa, stepped outside. It was twilight-dark although it was only four in the afternoon. We caught the bus to go downtown. We were all looking forward to the exciting New Year's Eve event. Small bonfires were planned at various places in Reykjavik, but the BIG one was down at a cleared field. The pile of wood from old or wrecked boats - old tires - anything burnable was, to me, scary-tall.

We found a good place to sit down on the ground and wait for the show to begin. I looked up into the dark-blue sky where a gazillion-trillion stars twinkled. In microseconds, that's one millionth of a second, there was a huge multicolored, spiral-curtain sparkling and moving very fast. Suddenly, purple and green streaked patches broke away from the curtain and leaped across the entire sky in an awesome show, for several minutes, then floated off and away...only to come back, move side to side in amazing display of bright colors that looked like fractured rainbows!

As the bonfire was lit and the huge pile was burning to the sky, people started dancing around in a huge circle, welcoming the New Year. Brennivín and coffee flowed generously.

People began belting out folk songs and singing at the top of their voices. I enjoyed the great spectacle, but thought that the Aurora Borealis was by far more impressive, and memorable, even though it's quite a frequent, and welcome, show during the long dark Icelandic winters.

It was our usual custom to go to our 'rich' Aunt's house on

New Year Day for dinner. Aunt Þrúður, mother's sister, and her husband Jón. They lived in a beautifully furnished place above their store. They had a PIANO! Kalli, my half-brother, turned out to be the musician in our family.

The steps in the foyer, leading to the upstairs, had a brass edge that Sísí, Lilla and I got to scrub, and polish to a mirror-like finish each time we visited. After we were through polishing we'd tiptoe, and admire, each elegant step all the way up to the top.

Jón always sat at the head of the table and Aunt Þrúður at the other end. After a scrumptious dinner of smoked mutton, creamed potatoes, boiled eggs, and other goodies, plus cream-torte for dessert, each of us kids went to our hosts. Extending out our right hand, first to our Aunt and then to Jón, we girls would put our right toe behind our left heel, bend our knees while holding unto the hem of our dresses with our left hand, and give them a nice curtsy, while Búddy and Frankel bent deep from their waist and bowed quite elegantly.

Búddy NEVER acted up at Aunt Þrúður's home!

Chapter 30

Jólasveinarnir
The Yule Lads

In preparation for Christmas we kids had done our traditional ritual; we each, had placed a pair of our shoes on the window-sill, starting December the 12th . Very carefully, we made sure that we were extremely good. I was super-careful. Mother had told us many stories about Grýla and her terrible tröll family, who liked to chase, and grab a hold of naughty kids.

The tröll couple had at least 13 sons, there were supposed to be many more but these were the ones that seemed to delight in causing mischief among folks. The sons started out trying to snatch naughty children and stick them into the huge black burlap-bag they had slung over their grotesquely lumpy shoulders. They would then take the naughty kids to their Monster-Mamma. [I tried to question this during a catechism lesson, but I didn't get very far. I got the 'LOOK'].

I never heard of any kids getting caught. They were either so good, or they could out-run the trölls.

Evidently, over the years the lads mellowed and became Christmas, or Yule-legends, and named Yule Lads. According to folklore; somewhere along the years they started leaving small presents in the shoes of the good kids. (We were, especially, thrilled if we got our own little candles)

But a piece of black lava-rock, or worse, a rotten potato would be in the shoes of the naughty children, as a reminder to be good. Just the thought of getting a rotten potato kept us kids behaving ourselves and anxiously checking our shoes.

These mischievous boys were not known for their good manners as their names indicate. How they had the nerve to leave rocks for naughty children when they themselves misbehaved was beyond me. But this was something I couldn't question either!

These are a few of the known names of the Jólasveinar, and their Poems;

Stekkastaur---Sheep-Cote Clod, the first Yule Lad comes to town December the 12th .The first of them was Sheep-Cote Clod...

> He came stiff as wood,
> to prey upon the farmer's sheep
> as far as he could.
> He wished to milk the ewes,
> but it was no accident
> he couldn't; he had stiff knees
> -not to convenient.

✳✳✳

Giljagaur -- December 13th came **Gully Gawk** (or Crevasse Imp) this lad likes to hide in gullies and wait for opportunity to steal milk.

> The second was Gully Gawk;
> grey his head and mien,
> He snuck into the cow-barn
> from his craggy ravine
> Hiding in the stalls,
> he would steal the milk, while
> the milkmaid gave the cowherd

a meaningful smile.

✳✳✳

Stúfur ---Shorty, or Stubby, the shortest of the brothers, arrived in the 14th.

> Stubby was the third called,
> a stunted little man,
> who watched for every chance
> to whisk off a pan.
> And scurrying away with it,
> he scraped off the bits
> that stuck to the bottom
> and brims - his favorites.

✳✳✳

Skeiðisleikir--- Spoon-Licker came down from the mountains on 15th of December.

> The fourth was Spoon Licker,
> like spindle he was thin.
> He felt himself in clover
> when the cook wasn't in.
> Then stepping up, he grappled
> the stirring spoon with glee,
> holding it with both hands
> for it was slippery.

✳✳✳

Pottaskefilll---Pot-scraper (or Pot-Licker) is expected on December the 16th.

Pot Scraper, the fifth one,
was a funny sort of chap.
When kids were given scrapings,
he'd come to the door and tap.
And they would rush to see
if there really was a guest.
Then he hurried to the pot
and had a scraping fest.

❋❋❋

Áskasleikir---Bowl Licker, came to town on December the 17th.

Bowl licker, the sixth one,
was shockingly ill bred.
From underneath the bedsteads
he stuck his ugly head.
And when the bowls were left
to be licked by dog or cat
he snatched them for himself
- he was sure good at that!

❋❋❋

Hurðaskellir---Door-slammer, came to town on December the 18th.

The seventh was Door Slammer,
a sorry, vulgar chap:
When people in the twilight
would take a little nap,
he was happy as a lark
with the havoc he would wreak,

slamming doors and hearing
the hinges on the squeak.

✳✳✳

Skygámur---Yogurt Gobbler---On the 19th Yogurt Gobbler
makes his appearance.

Yogurt Gobbler was the eight,
was an awful stupid bloke.
He lambasted the yogurt tub
till the lid on it broke
Then he stood there, gobbling
-his greed was well known-
until, about to burst,
he would bleat, howl and groan.

✳✳✳

Bjúgnakrækir---Sausage-Swiper---shows up on December
the 20th.

The ninth was Sausage Swiper,
a shifty pilferer.
He climbed up to the rafters
and raided food from there
Sitting on a crossbeam
In soot and in smoke,
he fed himself on sausage
fit for gentlefolk.

✳✳✳

Gluggagægir---Window   Peeper---This   one   starts   his
peeping on the 21st.

Íeda Jónasdóttir Herman

The tenth was Window Peeper,
a weird little twit,
who stepped up to the window
and stole a peek through it.
And whatever was inside
to which his eye was drawn,
he most likely attempted
to take later on.

✳✳✳

Gáttaþefur---Door Sniffer, he comes around December
22nd.

Eleventh was Door Sniffer,
A doltish lad and gross.
He never got a cold, yet had
A huge sensitive nose.
He caught the scent of lace bread
While league away still
And ran toward it weightless
As wind over dale and hill.

✳✳✳

Ketkrógur---Meat Hook---arrives on December 23rd. St.
Thórlák´s Day.

Meat Hook, the twelfth one,
his talent would display
as soon as he arrived
on Saint Thórláks Day.
He snagged himself a morsel

of meat of any sort,
although his hook at times was
a tiny bit short.

✳✳✳

Kertasníkir---Candle Beggar---came on December 24th. He longed to have his very own candle.

The thirteenth was Candle Beggar
-'twas cold, I believe,
if he was not the last
of the lot on Christmas Eve.
He trailed after the little ones
who, like happy sprites,
ran about the farm with
their fine tallow lights.

This popular poem about the Yule Lads was written by the late Jóhannes from Kötlum, and first appeared in the book "Jólin Koma" (Christmas is coming) in 1932.

Chapter 31

Random Memories March 1936
Bolludagurinn (Bun Day)

This was one wonderful, yummy holiday in gloomy winter, two days before lent. Every store, cafe, and other eating/meeting places overflowed with Bollur (buns), and folks stuffing themselves before lent. The delicious cream puffs were filled with custard, jams or dipped in chocolate.

We kids tried to get up before Mother got up from her bed and Gróa got up from the divan where she slept. We'd run with our brightly decorated wands, called Bolludagsvöndur or [Bun Day Wand], gripped tightly in our hands. As many times as we were able to swat them before they were out of bed, we'd get that many buns!

The following day was called Spreingidagur (Bursting Day). How appropriate!

ÖSKUDAGURINN.
(Ash Wednesday)

We had pieces of colorful fabric scattered on the floor and table. Gógó and I were doing the cutting, while Lilla held the fabric steady. Ása and Sísí were sewing.

White, red, green and black spools of thread were on a chair. A large red pincushion full of needles and straight-pins sat on the table. Next to the cushion lay a horseshoe-shaped magnetic bar, which we used to pick up any stray pins that found their way to the floor.

Öskudagurinn was the next day and we were frantically trying to finish at least a dozen Ösku-pokar [ash bags]. We had big ones, little ones, cotton ones, and silk ones. Some solid colors, some print.

Each bag had a small amount of ash placed in the bottom. A drawstring closed the top, and a four-inch long string was left hanging on which we fastened a straight pin that we bent in half, to form a hook. This we would then hang on the back of unsuspecting folks.

Several kids with the same purpose as we, were already downtown. All of us hid the bags in our sweaters and waited for our victims.

Some folks walking by had bags already dangling on their backs. Ása and Sísí went across the street and found a prime target right away. Lilla was too little to sneak up behind people and reach high enough to hook a bag on some-ones back so she carried my bags.

We got one great opportunity as a very dignified man walked past us. His long black overcoat made a perfect target. With pickpocket deftness, I was able to add onto his back two of the gaudiest, and largest, bags we had made. My sister got her chance; since the back of his coat almost reached to the top of his shoes, she was able to snag a small bag at the hem of his coat. It dangled splendidly at every stuffy step!

We were almost hysterical as we watched the gaudy bags swinging on the back of the pompous dignitary, who stalked ever so importantly toward the parliamentary building!

Lilla and I walked a few steps behind him and counted seven bags flip-flopping on his back. We were doubled up with laughter as Sísí and Ása ran up to join us in our giggles. What a fun day this had been!

In the days following, I thought back on those times, as reports on the situation in Europe steadily got worse. Rumors had it that German submarines were now in the North Atlantic, and were circling Iceland.

Chapter 32

World War II, 1939

Stories were beginning to be heard in Iceland how the power hungry Nazi leader of Germany, Adolph Hitler, was bent on conquering the continent. The superiority of the German army seemed unquestionable as they invaded country after country; Denmark, Sweden, Norway. Then France and the Netherlands were overtaken.

When the Nazi invaded Poland, an ally of Britain, the British entered the conflict and a full-scale conflict now raged in Europe. Iceland declared neutrality.

Father was still traveling to England and we were constantly on edge for his safety. Our remote country was not as immune to the war as I had once thought; reports of German submarines circling in the Atlantic off the Icelandic coasts intensified as the European war escalated.

Now, at the age of fourteen, I was on my way to Vopnafjörður (this turned out to be my last trip there.) We traveled with great trepidation and fear of the German submarines but arrived without an incident. Grandpa was at my Aunt's house to meet me, and he had everyone in an uproar, insisting that Ólafur check the whereabouts of Kristján, Finna's dad, to make sure that his, Grandpa's, and Kristján's paths wouldn't cross.

Rumor had it that several men, including Kristján were sympathetic to the Nazi party.

"I wouldn't put it past him and his cronies to be signaling the Germans off of Lánganes." Grandpa fumed. I never heard of that and spent an uneventful summer; first with my Aunt and then at Hámundarstaðir with my Grandparents.

Grandpa had his ears pretty much glued to the radio that was almost impossible to understand due to crackling and static. The information we were able to get were unsettling and between that, and Grandpa's tirade, I got quite uneasy about sailing back home in the fall.

But when that time came we arrived in Reykjavík without any trouble. The town was abuzz about grim reports on how Jews were being annihilated in gas chambers. We found that hard to believe, we knew the Germans to be good people, but it seemed that Hitler and the Nazi party were changing that.

We also heard a report that the Germans were building a new warship; the *Bismarck* with its eight 15" guns was the largest and the most advanced battleship built at that time. In 1940 the *Bismarck* was launched and soon became a terrible threat on the oceans.

Iceland was in a very strategic place between Europe and North America, and the Brits were getting concerned over Hitler's interest in Iceland. Britain was unable to get the Icelandic government to join them in a pact against Germany so they invaded our island. The North Atlantic soon became a battleground as the British chased the German warships, and submarines, that Hitler sent with orders - to destroy Allied convoys that were in transit to Britain.

In 1941 a fierce fight broke out in the Denmark straits - the ocean between Iceland and Greenland which became known as "Torpedo Junction" - and the *Bismarck* sank the battle cruiser *HMS Hood,* the pride of the British Royal Navy. Fourteen hundred and sixteen men went down with the ship. Prime Minister Winston Churchill promptly issued an order *"Sink the Bismarck!"* A relentless pursuit of the dreaded ship ensued. The

Germans, temporarily, got away from their hunters and headed for a safe port in France, but Torpedo planes from the British Royal Air Force got the notorious menace before it reached safety and sank it. Twenty five hundred German sailors drowned.

The United States had now entered into the war and Winston Churchill is said to have "slept the sleep of the saved and the thankful" because "there was now no doubt about the outcome of the conflict." It was no longer just a European war but had now become World War II and American service men and women were sent all over the globe.

As the war went on, Icelandic fishing boats were being attacked and sunk by the Germans. Then we heard that the trawler *Max Pemberton,* the ship Father had previously been on, disappeared without a trace in the Atlantic. Pétur Maack and his crew were presumed drowned.

Our family was in constant unease when Father was out at sea.

Even with the loss of several fishermen, Iceland maintained neutrality, but did make an agreement with the U.S Government to have Navy bases built there. The first troops arrived in our country shortly after the attack on Pearl Harbor in 1941. Most of the twenty five thousand Brits left and were replaced by forty thousand American Troops.

They, British and Americans, were not entirely welcome in our country as they outnumbered the, about, twenty thousand adult Icelandic males. The total population of the country was some hundred and twenty thousand at that time. Our Government frowned on the fraternizing of Icelandic women with the service men.

The U.S. did not allow their troops to marry, regardless of country they were stationed in. Both Iceland and the U.S issued a ban on marriage.

Eventually, even though the sailors were mostly confined to base, they did get to coffee shops and restaurants in town, causing a dating game to flourish. These American strangers were interesting; they spoke in a funny way. Laughing a lot, they seemed uncommonly cheerful. Quite different from the dour English and Scots.

Although not enthusiastically welcomed, the presence of the U.S. Troops gave a sense of "one could sleep the sleep of the saved..." as Churchill had said.

In Europe, the advances of the Nazi army were slowing down, and the Allies were gaining ground. Rumors were rampant about Hitler. He was said to be in Iceland because a plane had been spotted to drop something down on a small village on the eastern shore. People speculated that the infamous Fuhrer had been parachuted into the country.

U.S. Troops hunted for him where he was thought to be hiding, a place called Skríðuklaustur in Djúpivogur. People there called the idea "ludicrous". The folks were right, he was still in Berlin where he later hid in a bunker and took his own life in Spring of '45.

Chapter 33

Del Comes to Iceland, 1943

Seventeen-year-old Del stood shivering at the rail of the camouflaged troopship.

The biting north wind, mixed with rain and sleet, stung through his Navy Pea jacket like the piercing of dozen needles. Cupping his hands over the tip of his freezing ears, he squinted through the murky air. Morosely, he felt the ocean's slow heaves gently lifted the ship in hypnotic moves.

It had just been announced that the troopship was on its way to Iceland, and he had been told that's where he was being deployed. Sure wouldn't have enlisted if I'd known where I'd end up. Del dried a dribble at the end of his nose, as he, enviously, thought of his two brothers, who were somewhere in the South Pacific.

Of all the places in the world he could have been sent to, he had to go to a forsaken place called Iceland! Just the thought of it was enough to give one the chills. Del shivered again. As if that wasn't bad enough, he grumped to himself, they were now traveling in a strait named 'Torpedo Junction,' because of the fierce fighting going on between the Brits and the Germans, and the proliferation of German submarines circling the island like hungry sharks.

"Nasty weather!" Someone chuckled behind him. "Far cry from Illinois, where I am from." Continued the owner of the cheerful voice. A hand clapped Del slightly on the shoulder. "My name is Curtis, what's your name, mate?" Without waiting for an answer, he chuckled again. "Iceland! I can't imagine a worse place to be sent to."

Del turned in surprise, and exclaimed; "Illinois! Hey, what are the odds of that?" Reaching out and shaking the hand of a sailor, who looked to be about twenty.

"My name is Del, and I, also, am from Illinois!"

Grinning at each other as they reminisced about their hometowns, the ship continued its full steam ahead. (They couldn't have know that they would become close friends, and Curtis would end up in being the best man at Del's wedding to an Icelandic girl a year and a half later.)

Suddenly, Curtis pointed to a pod of orcas shooting up from the ocean.

"Have you ever seen anything like that?"

They were in awe as other sailors joined them to enjoy the show. After a few excited remarks, they fell quiet and stared at the horizon, where a massive, ice-covered, mountain range appeared.

As the ship sailed closer and entered the sheltered harbor Reykjavik, they were astonished to see rather modern-looking buildings, no highrises, but still a pleasant surprise.

"I guess I was expecting Icelanders to be living in igloos." Del, said, sheepishly.

"I was thinking the same thing." Curtis mumbled. "Maybe this won't be quite as awful as we had anticipated." He scratched his head and blurted." Frankly, what I see so far, the name 'Iceland' seems misleading." Then jumped as orders blared out. Time to go ashore.

A nice surprise awaited them; the Leathernecks who had arrived the year before had worked swiftly, and hard, with military smartness to build barracks in which the men had to live.

Camp Knox, as the base was called was on the edge of Reykjavik

Arriving in September, as they did, it took a while for Del and Curtis to get used to the gloomy days that stretched over winter as a one, long, dark, night. From noon, to about four in the afternoon it was like living in a twilight zone.

One day Curtis came running to Del and hollered.

"How about going to a dance tonight?" He waved a piece of paper into the face of his friend. "Marlene Dietrich, and troupe are going to be at White Rose Hall."

When Del started to shake his head, Curtis growled at him.

"Come on, it's spring let's celebrate!" After several urgings, Del reluctantly agreed to go. He was surprised that he actually was enjoying the evening. The actress' show was well received. She was not a great singer, but her sultry voice was intimate. She had a way of making the guys feel like she was singing for each one only.

Del scanned the crowd of service men when his eyes became riveted on the front entrance of the dance hall.

"Hey, Curtis, you've been here before, have you seen that girl before." Del nudged

"Who? Where?" Curtis craned his neck.

"At the door, the one with the long, dark hair, she's with the red-head and blonde." Del hitched his head in the direction of the three girls that were just coming in. Suddenly he made a beeline for the young girl, who had made a move as to leave. Almost colliding with her in his haste, he reached out.

"Dance?" He asked. "I'm not very good at it, but I'd like to dance with you." At her confused look, Del realized the girl's knowledge of English was limited. Quickly deciding fewer words were better, he gave her an entreating look, and merely said,

"Please?"

That much she understood, and said "Okay."

Dancing most of the evening with few words, Del was totally smitten. When he asked her to come back the next night, she agreed. It was a very happy, young man that went back to the base that night.

Chapter 34

Spring 1944 Del and I Meet

In 1944, in the capital of Iceland, Reykjavík, I met my husband to be, Del. He was in the United States Navy. Being color-blind, he was assigned to the "Sea Bee's" (the Construction Battalion). We both were nineteen years old. Two girlfriends of mine persuaded me to go downtown with them to an USO dance, at a place called White Rose Hall. As we entered, my two friends deserted me to meet their boyfriends.

All around me was loud chatter, mostly American accents, but mixed with few British and Scottish brogues. Feeling un-expectantly shy, knowing very little English, I turned to leave and almost collided with a young, very good-looking, dark-haired, slim sailor, who had a huge smile on his face.

"Dance?" He said something else that I didn't understand.

I shook my head.

"Please?" Something about that plea, and the entreaty in his soft hazel eyes made my heart do a flip-flop. These were difficult times no one knew who would come back when sent out on a mission; ships were torpedoed, airplanes were shot down and many service men were losing their lives.

"Okay." I knew that one word; it was as universal as "Coca-Cola". As we danced that evening, it was like we'd both been hit by a bolt of lightning! No need for words, just looks and - for me anyway - silly smiles.

We met again at the dance hall the next evening, and as we danced he asked me to marry him. I looked at him, thinking I knew what he was asking, but not quite sure. Del asked again, taking my left hand and acting like he was putting a ring on my finger. Then I knew, and said "yes." We were serious! The next day we told Mother.

"YOU WANT TO DO WHAT." My soft-spoken, easy going, Mother shouted! This was not good. Mother never raised her voice - not at us kids, not at my Father, no one. Now she had really raised her voice!

"Hermann and I want to get married." I repeated. (Later, in my family Del was always called Hermann, I guess it rolled easier of the tongue).

Mother had her face buried in both hands, rocking from side to side. She was quiet for a moment then she looked up, wide-eyed shock still on her face.

"Íedamín, will Hermann live in Iceland? Or, heaven forbid, are you going to move to Amerika? Do you realize how far it is? We don't know anything about his family. We don't even know what part of the country he's from. It's a huge country. You could get lost, then what?" Mother nervously twisted her fingers, then dabbed at her eyes with a hankie.

Del had been holding my hand and trying to follow a conversation he couldn't understand. He didn't speak Icelandic, and my mother didn't speak English. My English wasn't a whole lot better; we got by with hugging, kissing and holding hands! Del squeezed my hand. He could see that this wasn't going as well as we had hoped.

I said something like, "You home Amerika?" He looked at me a little puzzled. I tried again.

"You Mamma, home, Amerika?"

Del smiled that great smile of his and said: "Chicago"

Mother about fell off of the sofa, gasping. "Chi-ka-ga? Gangstar Chi-ka-ga?!?"

It didn't come out "gangster" but close enough. We had some explaining to do and it wasn't going to be easy!

As usual - in Icelandic households - the coffeepot was steaming. I got up and placed three cups and saucers on the table to give Mother time to get over her shock. As I poured the coffee, I grinned at Del, a little wickedly I'm afraid. I knew he detested the drink but would pretend to like it for the sake of being polite. You haven't tasted *coffee* until you've tasted the way we used to make it, strong enough for the teaspoon to stick straight up out of the cup! I put the sugar-cube bowl out and sat down as a grateful Del scooped up a handful of cubes.

After a while, Mother sighed and gracefully accepted the situation.

"Hermann is nice enough, Íedamín." Mother acknowledged, and then she shook her head and smiled. "Well, I guess I'd better get to know this young man of yours!" And that's how she took the news.

Father had been out at sea and when he came home, we shared the news. He was quiet but he also accepted our wishes.

Now that my parents had agreed to our marriage, it was time for Del to tackle the '"powers" that be. Wearing down layers of authorities by unwavering persistence, he got the ban lifted and was the first U.S. Service man to marry after that. On March 25, 1945 we were married in the *Dómkirkjan,* in downtown Reykjavík. Mother gave me away. Father was out at sea and was spared the embarrassment of being present when a daughter of his was marrying an army man. My two sisters attended, but not my brothers. Icelandic folks, especially men, were upset when girls started dating the "foreigners."

The church was full of various army personnel; American, English and Scots...most of them strangers to us. A virtual floodgate opened up as service men later rushed to tie the knot!

Mother was right, aren't mothers *always* right? What was I thinking? I knew next to nothing about America. Of course, I knew Leifur Eiríkursson had discovered America long before Columbus. I'd heard about New York, glamorous Hollywood where the famous stars in the movies lived and Chicago, where all the gangsters were.

Del said he didn't live in that city but in another one not too far away. How would I get there? Would I travel by myself like I would to New York? He had to stay in the Navy until fall, at which time he would be discharged.

"Not a problem," he said. "My mother will meet you in New York."

"Your mother drives a car?" I was impressed. In our town, we had buses and a few dilapidated "taxis." Otherwise we traveled by horses or ships.

"Mother doesn't drive." Del laughed." She'll take a train to New York, and you'll go back with her to Illinois on one." I'd never seen a train! Mind you, this was all carried on by many hand gestures, and 'pidgin-English' by me.

As time went on I learned more English words and I tried to teach Del Icelandic, without much success. We took walks, hand-in-hand, around the lake in the center of downtown Reykjavik. Del would point and say *"water"* I'd say *"vatn."* He would say *"birds,"* I'd say *"fuglar."* Although he just couldn't get THOSE pronunciations he did quite well with the words "Elska mín" translated "My Love. "

Coming from totally different worlds as we did, I had a fleeting doubt, and then pushed it away, I was in love.

Reykjavík , Iceland
March 25, 1945

Chapter 35

Coming to America

THE ENORMOUS, BATTLE-SHIP GREY, troop-transport, *USS Merak,* was anchored out in the bay, past the two flashing lighthouses that guarded the entrance to the harbor of Reykjavík. The ship had sailed in from Europe the night before. It was to leave early this morning.

Mount Esja had snow scattered across her top. The sharp wind was nippy and the billowing clouds whipped across the ice-blue sky. The sea moved in shallow heaves and sloshed against the ship. The huge hunk of metal barely moved.

It was June 6, 1945. I was standing on the pier with Mother, Sísí, Lilla and Del. My bags were already stored aboard the landing boat, with hundreds of assorted boxes and belongings of dozens of troops who were heading back home to the United States, after completing their tours of duty in Iceland. Unfortunately, my husband wasn't among them. We wouldn't see each other until September. I was going by myself to America. I'd never been out of this isolated island.

I was clueless.

The sailors hurried back and forth with the collar of their Navy pea coats turned up against the biting wind. It was time to go. Giving my family a hug, I boarded the boat that would take me out to the ship.

This time, unlike my previous journeys, there was no jumping, no shouting, just flurries of white hankies waved by Del, my Mother and two sisters, as the boat slowly veered away from the dock.

As we neared the gargantuan ship I felt the first twinge of unease, but then the boat went smoothly up to steps fastened at the side of the ship. Hands reached down, steadying me, holding mine with firm grips and guiding me to the deck. A smiling woman, with a Red Cross band on the arm of her U.S. Navy Uniform, guided me to the rail where I could look for my family. I could hardly see them because of the distance, and my eyes were now blinded with tears.

Suddenly, the noise of the ship's engines starting up. The ocean churned up like the cauldron of the Geysers as they roiled, bulged and boiled before erupting. *The USS Merak,* slowly, eased its way out of the harbor.

I stared a moment at Mt. Esja and the island of Víðey, then slowly turned and looked at the town of Reykjavík. My family was barely visible on the misty pier. When would I see my home again? Would I ever? Nausea squeezed through my stomach. I swallowed hard, watching the mountains and glaciers, slowly fade and blend with the sky and ocean on the eastern horizon. With mixed feelings of excitement, and unease, I saw my country disappear from my view. I shivered and wrapped my sweater tight around my shoulders.

On the north horizon, a long trail of black smoke from a trawler billowed into the sky and slowly blended with the grey clouds. Soon the ship faded out of sight. I wasn't aware how long I stood there looking on an infinite plain of undulating water.

A sailor gave me a soft tap on the shoulder saying.

"Food."

He said something else I didn't understand, but by his motion I knew to follow him to the dining area. This first day went fast - there were so many new and different things to learn, mainly trying to follow the language.

In the following days, I got to know the routine of breakfast, lunch and supper. The food was totally different than what I was used to, and the manner of dining even more so. To say that I felt out of place is putting it mildly. I was like a fish out of water!

The second morning I got up feeling tired. I hadn't slept well, tossing and turning all night with questions and doubts churning inside of me like wriggly worms. Listlessly, I took a shower and got dressed, skipping breakfast - not sure it would stay down with all the turmoil going on inside.

I decided I'd changed my mind. I didn't want to go to America after all. I didn't want to leave the only home I had ever known. But how in the world was I going to get back? I felt trapped. Grabbing a pillow, I scrunched it tight against my chest. After fighting utter panic for a few moments, I started scolding myself, like I used to do as a little child when terror gripped my heart.

"Come on, you're a grown married woman now... and where is your 'explorer spirit'?" I jeered at myself as I fought for control. I couldn't remember being this wretched since Hanna died. Why did I have to think of that? I was just a small child then; ten years ago, seemed more like hundred!

Miserable, I tottered up to the deck and leaned over the side of the rail. Nothing but ocean and sky met my eye. Suddenly, my heart started hammering at the sight of familiar white sprays shoot up into the air as a pod of whales cavorted in the ocean. Then two dolphins followed us. They swept up and down in the wide wake of the troopship. After a short time, they all turned and headed north.

All of a sudden, it was as if a line had been drawn in the water. The whales and dolphins were gone. There was nothing to see. They'd just said "Goodbye".

Turning in a complete circle, I stared where the sky met the sea. The horizon looked the same in all direction. I retreated below deck, emotionally spent.

The whole next day was spent reading and knitting. I had awakened suddenly in the early morning. For a moment I felt disoriented and wondered what I was sensing. Then I felt it - the ship was lifting up, up, up, hovering still for a moment before shuddering and groaning its way down, down, down - I looked through the porthole; the ocean was wild from roaring wind and driving rain. Going topside that day was of no interest.

The weather was much the same on day four. I meandered into the dining room where sailors, both men and women, were sitting at tables playing cards. Guitar music with sad-sounding vocals were coming from a Jukebox. I didn't understand the words, but the voice seemed heart breaking. Not needing that, I left. Back in my room and started aimlessly assembling my six-inch, crochet, squares together. I was half-way to making a full size bed throw for my mother-in-law.

On the fifth day of traveling on the Atlantic with nothing but ocean and the heavens, I noticed that the air was much warmer, the sky bluer, and the sun hotter. Even the sea was calmer than I was used to. Feverish activity aboard ship began. Everything was being 'spit' polished and shined. Whistling, smiling sailors began scrubbing and hosing down the deck with new enthusiasm and energy.

We would be arriving in America in the morning.

I was up at sunrise, eager, but at the same time very scared as I thought of what was ahead of me. The sailors had now changed into liberty whites and were lined up along the troopship's rail. The immense Statue of Liberty loomed magnificently against the cloudless, vivid blue sky. Her right hand thrust up into the air holding a beacon of light and her left hand clasped a book to her chest. Rows of the tallest buildings I had ever seen towered in the background. No mountains, just black and glass and one massive skyscraper after another. My jaws clamped tight. THIS was scary!

Since my passport and all proper papers were in order, there was no delay for me at the Ellis Island, Immigration Port. But I could see that some were not so fortunate; I looked at the masses of suitcases, boxes and children that were scattered about the motley crowd, huddled in long lines. Most of the men and women looked worn and tired, but some were smiling. A few had a hunted, frightened look. Maybe I thought that because I was now feeling really scared, but then I was met by a very friendly Red Cross lady, who patted my arm as she waved for a taxi for us. I felt a little better. We started to get in, but not before a reporter from a New York newspaper poised his pen over his notepad and hollered at me.

"What do you think of New York?" Stepping up a little closer, as the Red Cross lady tried to shield me.

"Too much hot." I mumbled as I stumbled into the cab.

And off we went, with the cabbie driving like a maniac. I was sure he was going to run over people that were just simply everywhere. Gritting my teeth, I clenched the side of my seat with both hands, my eyes riveted on the rivulets of sweat that ran down the side of his face. The heat was suffocating. When I left Reykjavik the temperatures had been in the lower 50s, beautiful, crisp June weather. I was tremendously relieved when the crazy driver pulled up in front of a tall building and stopped. Stepping out, I craned my neck trying to see the dizzying top. I couldn't. My head was spinning.

The driver got out of his cab and opened the door for us. Trembling, I cautiously stepped out as the driver opened the trunk to get out my bags. After setting them down, he wiped his face with a grimy hankie.

"It's hot enough to fry an egg on the sidewalk!" He grumbled. I thought I got the gist of what he was saying and instinctively lifted up my foot not wanting to step into someone's eggs!

The Red Cross lady asked how much the fare was and pulled out bills to pay the man. He carefully folded it up and placed it into a small black bag on the seat. Then she reached out and handed him extra money. I was aghast. By Icelandic customs, she was insulting the man by implying he couldn't take care of his family. I expected him to spit on the sidewalk and haughtily upbraid her; 'I can take care of my own, I don't need a hand-out!' Instead, he gave her a huge grin. Touching his cap, he repeated his thanks and stuck the money into his pocket. I couldn't believe my eyes; this was so different from how I'd been brought up. My mind was in turmoil and I began to feel like a zombie.

My mother-in-law was standing by the hotel desk and turned toward us as we entered. She was a very short woman, dressed in a bright, blue-flowered dress. Her light brown hair, pulled back into a tight bun, was slightly grey at the temples. Her light-blue eyes sparkled behind large, silver-framed glasses. The small, blue, flower on her white straw hat bobbed, as she, with a quick step and a wide smile, came up to me and gave me a tight hug.

"I'm Mary, Del's Mom. Everything will be alright." She said in a soothing voice.

I must have looked as terrified as I felt. She, of course, didn't speak Icelandic, and my English was still pitiful. Somehow, we managed to communicate with much babbling and pointing. I felt her kindness.

The three of us walked into the, rather elegant, dining room where waiters bustled about covering tables with white cloths. Chrystal vases with red flowers complimented the red velvet upholstered chairs. The window swags and drapes matched the red velvet on the chairs. I loved the look of the golden fringe and tassel tiebacks.

Mary picked up the menu and ordered a meat dish, she called it "meat-loaf," for the two of us. The Red Cross lady ordered fried CHICKEN! I was horrified when I saw her carefully pick up a chicken leg and scrape off a piece of the meat with her fork. I looked at Mary who had cut up her food like she was preparing to feed a baby! I sat there, dumbfounded. I had my knife in my right hand and the fork in my left, as I'd been raised. Just then, the Red Cross lady picked up the chicken leg and daintily took a bite. I tried not to stare, but furtively looked around to see if the other diners had seen this uncouth behavior! No one was looking. I sighed, embarrassed.

After saying goodbye to the Red Cross lady, Mary and I followed a young man who was thoughtful enough to carry my two large suitcases. We entered the tiniest room that, without warning, moved and shook under our feet. The metal grinding all around was as bad as the screeching of ships cables in a fierce storm. I held on with a white-knuckle grip while the little room groaned, swayed and rumbled toward the heavens.

I stared at the young man who was nonchalantly chewing gum. American soldiers had introduced Wrigley's chewing gum to Icelanders. Younger folks and kids loved it but were forbidden to chew it because it looked like "cows chewing their cud" the older folks said. Mary seemed equally at ease as the young man did in this weird surrounding. I began to relax as the moving room slowed down, stopped and the clanking door opened.

The young man opened the door to a room and set the suitcases down. Mary reached in her purse and gave the man money. I waited, curious this time. Sure enough, he had the same reaction as the cab driver - a big toothy grin and thanks!

This must be the way people do it over here.

Grandpa would fume, and Great-Grandpa would turn over in his grave!

Our room was like an oven. I went to get a drink out of water out of the tap, took a big gulp and gagged; it smelled like volcanic fumaroles, or rotten eggs! I spit it out and ran to the window to get fresh air. I looked down; the cars below looked like small toys. I felt light-headed. Trying to get my head together and the bad taste out of my mouth, I chewed on an old, dried piece of kleinur I found in my pocket. Comforted by the familiar taste, I pondered what I had gotten myself into; what kind of country is this anyway? How can people survive this putrid tasting water! Baffled, I looked at Mary. She seemed healthy enough.

Departing from New York City, we journeyed toward the American heartland of the Midwest. The first leg.

The troop train was equally scary. This was my first train ride - I had never even seen one before! Everyone on the train was dripping with sweat in the overpowering heat as we entered Grand Central Station in Chicago. There we switched to the train that took us to the train station in Bloomington, Illinois. Then, on the final leg of our trip, we took a bus to Mary's house on Franklin Avenue in Normal.

Finally, my long and arduous journey, eleven days in all, was over and I had arrived in my new homeland. The house was a small, one story, white painted home in a row of other similar homes in an older neighborhood. That evening I stood in the yard and looked around, familiarizing myself with my new surroundings.

Across the street from Mary's house was an Assembly of God Church. I was looking at the church and thinking how strange it was - almost middle of June and very dark outside. I was used to seeing part of the sun all night at midsummer. Then I saw these little sparks - like the embers shooting up out of a volcano - but I didn't feel any shaking of the ground. Something wasn't right. The church must be on fire!

I ran inside and tugged at Mary's dress. "Hey-you, kirkjan [church] fire, fire!" I stuttered. Still not used saying Mary or mom, so I often called her 'Hey-you.' I pulled her to the front door and pointed. The sparks were even thicker than before and coming dangerously close to us!

"Fire?" She stared out and then looked at me, puzzled. "Where? I don't see any fire." She cocked her head at me, trying to understand my fear.

Frantically, I pointed. "See there, there!" I was twenty and acting like a six year old.

Turned out this was my first encounter with fireflies. Bugs with their own lights! Startling, and scary, I thought as I watched these little sparks land in grass and bushes, and not starting any fire. Del's Mom had quite a time educating me.

About three weeks later it was 4th of July. When I stepped outside of Mary's house, all up and down the street American flags were flying; big ones with halyards on poles which were landscaped around in the middle of immaculate, green lawns, small ones lining the walks, flags in every window, on the mailboxes, in children's hands, flags everywhere! We Icelanders love flying our flags, and do so at every opportunity. I was extremely happy to see that the American people felt the same about their flag. This will be a great country to raise a family, I thought as I walked back into the house and a new beginning. I was beginning to feel at home in America.

A few years later, I became an American officially. August 22, 1956 was a proud day for me. In Peoria, Illinois, I was administered the oath and sworn in as a *CITIZEN OF THE UNITED STATES OF AMERICA!* At that time, I was thirty and a mother of five.

As a citizen of Iceland, I enjoyed the odd beauty of my country; the mountains, the glaciers, and the fjords, yes, even the eruptions of awesome volcanoes.

As a citizen of the Beautiful and Amazing United States of America, it has been my pleasure to travel from the West Coast at the Pacific, to the East Coast at the Atlantic and from the north, at the Canadian border, to the southern tip of Florida, the Florida Keys, and through many States in between.

As a citizen of Heaven for almost sixty years, I am looking forward to the day I will get to explore and enjoy this, most beautiful country of them all...

Oh Lord my God
When I in awesome wonder
Consider all
The works Thy Hand hath made
I see the stars
I hear the rolling thunder,
Thy power throughout
The universe displayed.

When Christ shall come
With shouts of acclamations
And take me home
What joy shall fill my heart!
Then I shall bow
In humble adoration
And there proclaim
"My God how great thou art!"

Carl Gustaf Boberg, 1859-1940

EPILOGUE

Appendix A - Perils at sea; Father loses trawler *ICELAND II*.

Appendix B - Hard times in Eyjafjörður, from the diary of Sveinn Þórarinsson, magistrate´s clerk, 1869.

Appendix C - Earthquake in Dalvík, 1934.

Appendix A

Perils on the Sea

For Centuries the sea has been a generous giver of life to Icelanders as well as other countries around the world. Yet at times, terribly cruel, cold, and dreadful to the seaman who's life and love is the ocean. For the countries in the northern hemisphere, blinding winter snowstorms can come up without warning and turn the ocean into a merciless enemy.

My father, Jónas Björnsson, was passionate about the sea, calm or roaring, it was his life. Not only did he fish around Iceland, but also England and Canada. Among the fishermen he was fondly called *"King of the Fishermen"*. He had an uncanny ability to know where the fishing was best and set many catch-records on the east coast of Canada.

*The cruelty of the ocean caught up with the trawler in the horrible winter storm of 1967. The week that started Monday, February 20th, was one of the most tragic and terrifying ever known to fishermen. Early morning on February 21st, a trawler, *Cape Bonnie*, went aground on Woody Island, Newfoundland, Canada. All of the 18-man crew aboard perished. Prayers went up "for all those in peril on the sea... "as other ships were in danger from the brutal winter storm.

Desperate search was on for the Lockeport long-liner *Polly and Robbie*, but only the side of the deckhouse with a life-ring bearing the name *Polly and Robbie* was ever found. Seven more had now perished.

The *Iceland II* had left North Sidney, Cape Briton Island, on Sunday, February 19th, after unloading a cargo of fish. On her way back to the fishing grounds, she became trapped in ice off Glace Bay and didn't get free until late afternoon on the 20th. On the 23rd when the storm hit, with winds reported up to 100 miles an hour, the *Iceland II* went off course and slammed into the rocky shore near the village of Fourchu, Prince Edward Island, where the wreck was discovered. Later, two dories and a rubber raft were found on the rocks nearby. Ten more names were now added to the awful list.*

Father had gone to Iceland for New Year's Day and turned the ship over to a Canadian captain. At age 77 his ship gone, his crew dead, he never went back. He lived to the age of 96.

*Information gathered from The Canadian Fisheries Museum of the Atlantic Nova Scotia correspondent: Bonnie Purdy.

Trawler *ICELAND II* Went Down, Crew Drowned.
(Translated from the "Morning Paper", Reykjavik, Iceland - Tuesday 28, February 1967.)

Trawler owner Jónas Björnsson lost another ship 3 year ago and now considers quitting fishing. A tragic accident at Cape Breton, Nova Scotia last Saturday when the trawler *Iceland II* went down with the crew, ten men, drowned. Late Saturday men noticed that the trawler was stranded. Due to weather the rescue crew could not do anything, they had both boats and a helicopter. Sunday the bodies were found.

The Morning Paper contacted Jónas Björnsson the owner of the trawler who is here in Iceland now, some of his children live here. This is what he had to say:

---The trawler Iceland II was a 200 t. I came home to Iceland on New Year's Day and then the captain was waiting for the weather to change. He was going to leave after New Year's Eve but the weather was bad for many days. The crew consisted of rather young men, the captain was 35 years old, and they were both family men and single. I do not have much to say about who were hired on the ship, the captain did that. He was my first man last summer. There might have been some changes with the crew since I sailed with them.

---Yes, I have been in the trawler business 7-8 years. I went west in 1957. My first trawler, *Iceland I*, sank because of ice three years ago. The crew was rescued. It was steered towards land. I know very little about the accident with *Iceland II*. I phoned last night but could not reach those who are at the scene and the information I got is very little, except that last Friday the captain on *Iceland II* told another captain that they were going to harbor in Lais City. Everything was ok onboard. That is the last that was heard from the ship whatever happened after that.

---I do not know of any Icelanders onboard. I had an Icelander in my crew for two years but he left six months ago.

---I started in the trawler business in 1954. The trawler *Iceland II* was built in 1964 Bathhurst, New Brunswick. Last winter I was not fishing and therefore came to Iceland over the New Year. After this incident, I do not think I will continue in the business.

It has been very windy by the coast of Nova Scotia and Newfoundland all last week. 18 crew members were killed when the trawler *Cape Bonnie* went down last Thursday in St. Lawrence Bay. Also two small fishing boats are missing since last Wednesday. On these boats there were seven people.

Appendix B

Íslandssöguvefurinn: Vesturfararnir.
The Icelandic Immigration.

Hard Times in Eyjafjörður (Akureyri)

From the diary of Sveinn Þórarinsson, magistrate's clerk, 1869

✳✳✳

One cause of the mass migration West, was the brutal climate conditions during the 1860s. The following is an excerpt from the diary of Sveinn Þórarinsson, magistrate's clerk, detailing the effects of the severe weather at that time. From Sveinn it is possible to trace a path to the New World. Sveinn was the father of Jón Sveinsson, called Nonni, an internationally known children's book author from the early part of the twentieth century.

Sveinn Þórarinsson was a gifted man, a carpenter and bookbinder, a lover of music, a talented writer, an aesthete and connoisseur of many things. The following portion of his diary spans the period from May 24th to June 24th, 1869. The diary ends on the tenth of July of the same year; Sveinn died only a few days later.

✳✳✳

May 24. Frigid northerly breeze. The Pollur inlet is becoming choked with ice. Everywhere news of people near death; starving men slaughter starving sheep to save their own lives. Domestics wander from farm to farm begging for work in return for food and shelter. There is a general exodus of farmers in Skagafjarðasýsla and Þingeyjarsýsla. A general census meeting was held here today: I was present for part of it. Páll Magnússon and Ólafur from Espihóli came by. Before they left, I gave Ólafur and P. Johnson a chunk of snuff to chew. Men complain of sore throats and other physical woes due to lack of tobacco.

May 25. Hellish north wind, snowstorm. The ground white with snow down to the sea. I got 17 Pollack from Johnsen for two inches of snuff. Chopped a tree for firewood, made a table for the dormer window. I´m running out of hay for the cow. Polar ice filled the inlet and grounded six shark boats that were lying there.

May 26. Calm but frigid weather at first, then chilly southeast winds for a while. Polar ice floating at the bottom of the fjord. Walked into town and up to Eyraland in search of hay, but to no avail. Hung a couple of bundles of small herring to dry. Elin Gunnarsen moved here into the north end of my house. They began laying the footpath to the church. People are hoeing every square inch of their garden in a frenzy of hope and hopelessness.

May 27. Northwest snowstorm, freezing gale-force winds. I did some repair but then had to lie in bed for a long time due to the cold; no fires anywhere for the lack of firewood. I got three barrels of hay for one Danish dollar and 56 shillings and got temporary relief from that problem. Ever-increasing shortages and general scarcity of food. Total lack of coffee and tobacco everywhere; no victuals to be had except what little we can get from the sea. Havsteen, the merchant has nothing but moss and old tobacco slime in place of snuff; men use any and all kinds of surrogates for tobacco and coffee. I still have some tobacco left, and a little bit of food - dolphin meat and blubber, fish, beans, grains - but only enough for a few days. Others are no better off. I drink coffee made of beans and grain; sweeten it with molasses, which is still available. My cow only milks about 2.5 litres now.

May 28. Southwest gusts, slightly less cold. Northwest wind out of the fjord. Ice floating here at the bottom of the fjord again and gathering at Hrísey Channel. Our fishing nets catch nothing. I fixed my tools and workbench, then walked down with a bite of snuff for P. Johnsen, half out of his mind for lack of tobacco. Church path is finished. All ships on their way here, and others besides, get stuck in the ice on the east coast (Gunnólfsvík, Berufjörður). Norwegians have arrived at Seyðisfjörður full of pomp and self-importance.

May 29. Icy northwest gale. Fog. Fjord full of ice all the way to Leira. I made some wooden lids, a mousetrap, and a few other things during the day. Provisions are virtually exhausted by now in homes; no victuals left in stores. I sent Havsteen the merchant a little cut of snuff wrapped up in a cornet.

June 3. Northern windstorm, intermittent gusts of fog. Ebb tide pushes the ice further out of the fjord a bit though. I stayed home, puttered around, cured some herring. Starvation and the lack of hay are the news from all directions: it's said today that two children are dead of hunger in Ólafsfjörður. The snow is so deep in Fjörður and out in the surrounding countryside that only bare patches can be seen in the fields.

June 4. Cold northeasterly breeze. The air foggy and threatens snow. Couldn't work much because of the cold. Walked into town apothecary, bought a pound of chocolate and licorice and some dandelion root.

June 5. Devilish northeastern gale and snowstorm. Snow blanketed the ground down to waterline. I couldn't work. Sawed my last log for firewood and had to lie in bed to escape the cold. All my firewood gone. A couple of men rowed out yesterday and came back with a pitiful catch.

June 6. Calm clear weather, but still very cold. Árni Sólvason came from Þistilfjörður, having been on board the boats that are stuck in Finnafjörður on their way here and can't move because of ice around Lánganes. Several of us here in town sent a man to Vopnafjörður for tobacco. I put in 60 shillings for ½ pound of snuff. Yesterday I cut the last smidgen of tobacco that I owned. No fish to be caught; the nets drag nothing. Hunger closes in on us all, rich and poor alike.

June 7. Warm southwesterly wind. Most of the ice streamed out of the fjord, kindling hopes that a ship might come. Ólafur from Espihóli came, wanting to buy barley, but it wasn't available any more than anything else; finally he managed to get the last of some rye that had gotten soaked in kerosene. Several people have bought it for a Danish dollar a bushel out of sheer desperation. I figured out that the best way to cure my herring was to smoke it a little after marinating it in brine. Cows are being let out for the first time in the neighborhood, but I kept mine inside. Everyone has begun planting potatoes.

June 8. Northwest gale-force winds with cloudy streaks in the sky.

June 9. Still weather, warm and cloudy early in the day; southerly winds by evening.

June 10. Southerly gale force winds, but northwesterly winds high in the sky. Seemingly calm at the mouth of the fjord. By now, everyone is close to perishing from hunger. Many have begun slaughtering their stock to save their lives. No hope of ship's arrival at this time.

June 11. Hellish northerly gusts with intermittent snowstorms. Cows inside again, mine starving-hungry. Heavy snowfall. Conditions worsen steadily. I begged my way to ½ pound of juniper berries to eat. Lay in bed mostly due to the cold.

June 13. Northern frostbite gale. Ice ran all the way to Sigluvík. The cold is unbearable. Hunger sharpens. The magistrate and a couple of others from Möðruvellir came here and went home again. It is said that the magistrate got some grain from Möller, that both Möller and Steincke have several casks of meat, bread, and grain, which they are hoarding while death from starvation threatens all around them. I got a barrel of lousy hay from Friðjórn Steinsson for the cow.

June 14. Northern blizzard. Mountains snow-white. I was forced to kindle to stay alive. Ice thick all the way into Leira. A courier came from Siglufjörður to fetch the sheriff. The ship *Iris* from Hofsós was stuck there in the ice; *Rachel* lay in a hole in the ice out beyond Siglufjörður and couldn't move. The barque that was to come here lay in ice out by Höfðastekkur; Möller the merchant rode out immediately to get news of it, while Steincke sent out to Siglufjörður for news of *Rachel*. Blizzard winds and heavy snow during the evening. I got a half-barrel of foul hay from Apothecary Ó. Þórarensen for the cow. Magnús came from Vopnafjörður with tobacco. I got ½ pound of snuff.

June 15. Bitter northern gale; skies heavy as mid-winter. I heard that the last barque turned around and sailed back East, so Möller the merchant came home last night. I sat, updating the election records, sick from hunger. I haven't had any food other than a little plaice and salt-fish for a very long time. Eggert Gunnarsson was here in a fury trying to ensure that the people from Skagafjörður could get to the shipwreck in Siglufjörður. Dolphins in a hole in the ice at Oddeyrarbót. Men were chasing them and managed to get a few. Cows were let out door for a while today.

June 16. Clear and sunny; warm southwesterly breeze. The news is that the barque got trapped in the ice near Hvanndalabjarg and is in danger. Möller sent a request to Sigurðurat Boggverstaðir to get news of it. The ice floated out of the fjord as far as Höfði

June 17. South breeze, warm weather. Calm out in the fjord. Traces of westerly winds in the clouds. It rained in the evening for the first time this spring. I lay feeble and starving in my bed for most of the day. Had nothing for food except a bite of salt-fish and some fried fish skin, nothing to drink except some wild thyme water. The ice is mostly out at the mouth of the fjord now. Various reports of ships out beyond. I gave Þórleifur Bjornson a chunk of snuff.

June 18. Still, calm weather; warm thick air. This morning the sheriff's horses were sent from Svarfarðardalur, accompanied by notice of the auction of goods on the shipwrecked *Íris* on

Monday the 21st of this month. The sheriff had sent the magistrate grains, coffee, and a keg of spirits, and so it seems that Herod and Pilate are becoming friends again. Friðbjörn Steinsson sent his wife a pound of coffee, and I got a taste of it. The men from here decided to go to the auction in two boats; I went with Steinn's boat, for Björn the editor gave me bread and sausage (rúllupylsa) to eat on the way. I prepared for the trip as well as I could. The barque was said to have been seen in the ice at Látrar.

June 19. Still, sunny and hot at first, then a sea breeze, I waited for my travel companions out beyond Siglufjörður until 12:00, and we embarked in Steinn's boat in light winds. Reached Hjalteyri at 3, Syðstibær on Hrísey at 8, the cape of Ólafsfjörður at 11, lake Hvannadalsvatn at 12, approaching Héðinsfjörður at 2, and landed at Ýtrikrókur on Siglunes at 3, after rowing along the coast for fifteen hours, through the ice which virtually blankets the sea along the entire northern coast of the country. We landed the boat, offloaded, pitched tents, and got a little bit of rest. News today is that the barque *Emma* lay fast in a plate of ice out beyond Mána Islands. The stranded *Íris* lies here far from land, mostly sunken, with sea-soaked food and other provisions all over the beach, spread out on a sail.

June 20. Calm and very warm. We walked to Siglunes to get some coffee; what we got was thin and poor. Then Ólafur from Espihóli walked in over Skríður (stony and gravel slopes) into town, but I didn't feel up to accompanying him. The sheriff and Snorri the merchant came out to the headland to prepare the auction. At midday, I got a ride to Eyri on a little boat. *Rachel* lies there in the harbor along with several shark boats. I stayed the night in town with Ólafur and several others. Did some drinking during the evening. Jón Mýrdal showed me around.

June 21. Warm, foggy and still. The fjord of Siglufjörður is entirely choked with ice. I went with a few others out to Siglunes in a skiff; sometimes we had to drag the boat over the ice. We decided that Fríðbjörn Steinsson should bid at the auction as our proxy. The auction began, but Fríðbjörn did not do well by us. We got both fewer and more expensive things than necessary. The throng here is immense, most of them hungry people who constantly boil sea-soaked grains and shovel it, half raw, up into their mouths with shells, sticks, or whatever else they might find. We lay wet and exhausted in our wreck of a tent during the night. I slept little.

June 22. Cold, rainy easterly breeze. Auction continued today and ended at 4. We loaded the boat and embarked for Siglunes at 9:00, threaded our way along the coast in zig-zag pattern due to the pack of ice and other obstacles, came to Hrísey and were able to sail along Árnarnesnafir, reached Akureyri at 6 p.m. on the 23rd, after a 21-hour trip.

June 23. Sea breeze with light fog. We immediately divided up most of what we had bought and went to sleep. Ólafur from Espihóli went home. The last few days there have been good catches of whiting, Pollack, herring and plaice, which has greatly eased the severe hunger and helplessness of all here.

Credits:
Editors: Víðar Hreinson and Jón Karl Helgason.
Text author: Víðar Hreinson
English translation: Verba-Translation.

Appendix C

Earthquake in Dalvík 1934

As recorded in the *"Öldin Okkar"* (*"Our Century"*)

On Saturday the 2nd of June at 12:42 p.m local time a quick earthquake shook Eyjafjörður. It is thought to have been at 6,2 to 6,3 on Richter scale. The earthquake was noticed from Búðardalur in the west to Vopnafjörður in the east. It has been called the Earthquake of Dalvík for it was the most powerful in that area. This is the biggest earthquake remembered in this region. The source of the quake is thought to have been about 1 km east of Dalvík. Only the inhabited area nearest to the source was ruined.

The first shock was the longest and the strongest and followed by such noise that people thought it was an explosion. But they soon realized that it was an earthquake because houses trembled and things were thrown about. They were damaged or even destroyed. 'This shock must have lasted a minute and a half." (Öldin okkar 1931 - 1950bls.47) People ran out of their houses when the disturbance began, but sometime it was impossible because exits and doors were stuck; still no lives were lost.

Sigurður Þórarinsson, then a geology student, thought the quake occurred at an apt time, when people were eating and less exposed to danger. Everything was thrown about, windows broke, walls cracked, split an fell. Great cracks formed and indicated that the source of the earthquake was in Böggvistaðarfjall in the west of the village. The disturbance was such that potatoes recently planted were tossed up. Following are a few narratives;

Bjarki Elíasson, later a superintendent in Reykjavík, was a child when the earthquake began: *When I came home to Víkurhóll the whole house and the hill it stood on was cracked. My grandparents lived upstairs but my grandfather was blind and bedridden. People were helping him out when I arrived. My father was not at home, he was working as a carpenter in Svarfaðardalur. I went to fetch him on my bicycle because I thought he did not know about the earthquake. I did not get further than to the new primary school because of a crack in the road. I did not dare cross it. There I stood crying when my father came on his bicycle. When we came home my father went quiet, observed the damages and said: "This is a bad sight, the house will not be inhabitable again.*

In the year 1965 an article on the earthquake appeared in the Christmas edition of *"Dagur"* by Hjörtur E. Þórarinsson. "When the earthquake began he was in the sheep-cote at Tjörn. He stood in the doorway when the quake began. He heard a loud din and felt in an instant that the earth was moving under his feet, first slowly but then more violently. It was as he was standing on a carpet two men were pulling back and forth. A loud noise came from the roofs. He saw two boys who were working in the sheep-cot slipping their feet, then he fell. This disturbance only lasted a few seconds. He looked up to the mountain and saw the snow was now striped of mudslides. Everything went quiet but he felt that the peace was treacherous and he wished that the wind would increase or at least it would rain.

In *Öldin Okkar* 1931 - 1950 is written: In a house in Dalvík a woman had just given birth to her child. This house made of stone was greatly damaged. A wall collapsed and splinters from it fell over the woman in her bed but she and her baby were unharmed. Her calmness is thought to have helped a great deal.

In the mouth of Eyjafjörður ships were endangered. One captain said there was a sudden blow on his ship and that the crew below ran on deck because they thought the ship had stranded. Gigantic waves rose and seemed from the ship to be as tall as the mountains. The shock was the strongest in Dalvík and the damage according to that. The scene was terrible after the quake.

People hardly knew what hit them but soon they started to rescue things out of their houses, which were more or less damaged, half collapsed or cracked. Gables had fallen in some houses and open cracks were visible, but even so most roofs were still in place. It was too risky to enter some of the houses because they could collapse anytime. Inside them, almost everything breakable was smashed all over the place. Fireplaces were displaced and chimneys were broken. One house was caught on fire because of that.

After the incident when people had realized what had happened they went calm and more accurate in the rescue. Generally, people were very calm. One could expect more strong shocks and people wanted to save more from the houses before they would totally collapse.

During the night, the inhabitants tried to get as comfortable as possible. About 200 people were homeless because it was not presumed safe to sleep in the houses if further earthquakes would occur. After the first shock, the quakes were constant for the next hours. Therefore, people made their homes in sheds and tents.

Neighbors from nearby areas came and tried to assist as much as possible. The weather was nice which made everything easier. Crockery and other equipment for the kitchen were damaged so handling of food was particularly difficult. A week after the first shock, aid came from everywhere due to the government's encouragement.

GLOSSARY

A, Á

Akureyri; Second largest town in Iceland, situated in the north.

B

Breiðifjörður; Wide fjord (bay), west Iceland

D, Ð (say soft 'th')

Djúpivogur; Deep Cove

E É

Eldfell; Fire Mountain

Eyjafjallajökull; Island Mountain Glacier.

Eyjafjörður; Island Fjord

F

Flatey; Flat Island

Færeyjar; islands situated in the Atlantic Ocean between Iceland and Norway.

G

Gullfoss; Golden Falls

Goðafoss; The Falls of The Gods.

H

Heimaey; Iceland's largest island

Helgafell; Holy Mountain

Höfn; Harbor

I Í

Ísafjörður; Fjord of Ice

J

Jökullsár; Glacier River

Jökullsárlón; Glacier River Bay.

K

Kría; Arctic tern.

L

Lagarfljót; Lake Handsome.

Lagarfljótsormurin; The Worm of Lake Handsome.

Lögberg; Law Rock (situated at Þingvellir)

Lækjartorg; Down-town square Reykjavik

M

Mývatn; Midge Lake (no mosquito in all of Iceland!)

Mýrdalsjökull; Glacier of Mýrdal

P

Papey; Pope (or Monk) Island

R

Reykjavik; Capital of Iceland

Reyðarfjörður; Red (?) Fjord

S

Snæfellsjökull; Snow Mountain Glacier

Smörfjell; Butter Mountain

Siglufjörður; Fjord of Sails.

Skjálfandi: Trembling (shivering) Bay

V

Vatn; Water.

Vatnajökull; Glacier of Water.

Vestmanneyjar; West Men Island

Vopnafjörður; Fjord of Weapons

Þ (say hard th)

Þing; Parliament

Þingvellir; Old time meeting place of Parliament, congress.

Æ (say "I")

Æðarfugl; Eider bird (Eider duck).

Ö

Öræfarjökull

About the Author

Íeda Jónasdóttir grew up in Iceland, a country often called *The Land Of Fire And Ice.*

In 1944, at age nineteen she attended a USO dance and met an American service man, Del Herman, stationed in Reykjavik. They eventually married and after WWII, she came to the United States, where she and her husband made their home in Illinois. Over the years they became parents of three boys and seven girls that Íeda enjoyed entertaining with many folk-tales of her mysterious homeland. The children were especially intrigued with stories of the *'Hidden People'* who were known to be helpful folks, but did not take kindly to naughty children climbing on top of lava rocks that were known to be the *'Hidden's'* castles!

Íeda's love and creativity in decorating her home on a small budget inspired her to enroll at Chicago School of Interior Design. After graduating, she owned and operated her own design shop. Ms. Herman wrote numerous decorating articles that were published in local newspapers and magazines. She also prepared a handbook; *How To Decorate With Sheets And More*, which was made available at the numerous seminars at which she spoke: schools, women's clubs and church groups.

After retiring in 2009, and her family grown, Íeda's writing on decorating lead to writing her memoir for her family; *Trölls - Monster Worm - Hidden People.* Not one to stop there, Íeda enrolled, and graduated from the Institute of Children's Literature, West Redding, Connecticut.

Other Books by Ieda Jonasdottir Herman
The Silver Arrow Illustrated
Inner Space Aliens (2017)
Viking Kids Don't Cry (2017)

Co-Authored with Heidi Herman
Homestyle Icelandic Cooking for American Kitchens

CPSIA information can be obtained
at www.ICGtesting.com
Printed in the USA
FFOW03n1415130517
35431FF

9 780998 281650